THE GREAT CORNISH FOOD BOOK

A collection of recipes, tales and morsels from the ocean, fields and cliff tops of Cornwall

Editor: Ruth Huxley
Project Managers: Louise Searle, Steve England
Assistant Editors: Dave Huxley, Rosie Land
Copy Editors: Rachel Wilson-Couch, Melodie Manners
Designer: David Alcock
Assistant Designer: Alistair Marshall
Illustrator: Dawn Sheridan
Principal Photographer: Mike Searle
Contributing Photographers: Bob Berry, James Bowden, David Griffen, Steve Haywood, David Loftus, Greg Martin, Mike Newman, James Ram, Paul Watts, Bob Whitrow, Lisa Woollett

The Great Cornish Food Book:
A Muse Media production on behalf of Cornwall Food & Drink Ltd
Published by: Cornwall Food & Drink Ltd
Printed by: Fourway Print Ltd, Launceston, Cornwall

www.cornwallfoodanddrink.co.uk

Cornwall Food & Drink

PAGE 24: ORIGINAL RECIPE FROM *RICK STEIN'S FISH* FIRST PUBLISHED BY BBC BOOKS IN 1996 PHOTOS PAGE 23 © REBECCA BERNSTEIN, ANNA MCCARTHY

PAGE 32: ORIGINAL RECIPE FROM *NATHAN OUTLAW'S BRITISH SEAFOOD BY NATHAN OUTLAW*, PUBLISHED BY QUADRILLE (£25) PHOTO © DAVID LOFTUS

European Agricultural Fund
for Rural Development
Europe investing in rural areas

defra
Department for Environment
Food and Rural Affairs

CONTENTS

FOREWORD

There was a time when, if asked what they thought of when they heard the words 'Cornish food', people conjured images of scones and clotted cream or pasties. Nothing wrong with that! However, these days Cornwall can offer so much more; a whole range of dishes, which are not only available in shops, restaurants and eateries throughout the county, but are also made from ingredients that have, very often, been produced locally.

Cornwall is a magical place and its unique micro-climate means that things grow here that wouldn't grow in other areas of the UK. The mild climate that we enjoy means that our crops are ready first. The amount of rain we have means that cattle are able to graze on lush grass and that, in turn, means they produce the very best quality meat and dairy products. Around our coast, we have excellent fishing and can boast some of the best quality seafood and fish in the world. In all, Cornwall's natural larder means that, on our doorstep, we have all the ingredients necessary to produce the very best gastronomic delights.

It can be of little wonder then that Cornwall has become a magnet for chefs and cooks of the highest calibre, or that we have a healthy supply of talented, locally trained young chefs coming up through the ranks. Nor can it be denied that we have producers, fishermen and farmers who are equally talented and committed to producing the very best that Cornwall can offer. The enthusiasm that is felt by those working in and around the industry in Cornwall has made its mark on the gastronomic world and Cornwall is now seen as a hub of culinary excellence.

Cornwall Food & Drink are the dedicated team who bring together people from all walks of life but with one common interest – a love of, and respect for good Cornish food. The Great Cornish Food Book, a compilation of dishes from chefs who are currently at the top of their profession in Cornwall and stories of the people who produce the fantastic ingredients we work with, is bound to be a 'must have' for any lover of good food. I can honestly say that I count myself blessed to be a chef in Cornwall and proud to be a part of this book.

Happy cooking!

Nathan Outlaw

ROB WHITROW PHOTOGRAPHY

Like millions of other people, my earliest memories of Cornwall hark back to family holidays by the sea. My dad worked in the boatbuilding trade and he used to suss out the good holiday spots on his business trips. Padstow was his Cornish choice and the 150 mile journey from our home in Somerset took the whole of a very long day. If we arrived without breaking down it was always a bonus.

We adored Padstow. The best bit was trekking off with my brother and sister, just the three of us and our dog, discovering completely empty sandy coves and playing and exploring to our hearts' content.

There were two culinary highlights of those holidays: supper at the Clipper Restaurant (our posh treat) and cooking fresh crab back at our fisherman's cottage. The good old Clipper is still there on the front and always raises a smile when I see it. Anyone looking for a special treat these days is overwhelmed with so much more choice, such is the transformation that has taken place in the area's food scene over the intervening years.

We all used to join in with the picking of the crab, a ritual that started my passion for this unmistakable taste of the seaside. Little did I know then that some thirty years on, in the year 2000, I would be moving to Cornwall to bring up my own family here, and married to a man who can catch, cook and pick a crab like a pro.

Back then, despite being a confirmed foodlover, Yarg was the only Cornish cheese I could name, I didn't know how to serve a Cornish cream tea (in Somerset we used to put the cream on the bottom) and proper pasties were a revelation to me. Cornish food was something of a well-kept secret, largely retained within the confines of the Tamar.

I sometimes have to pinch myself to believe how much things have changed since then. Ask anyone nowadays what they love about Cornwall and more often than not 'the food' will be one of the first things they think of. Moreover, they will probably be able to reel off the names of Cornish products or places to eat that have become favourites in their household. The Cornish food revolution of the 21st century has seen a once limited range of produce become one of the most diverse to be found anywhere. There are

examples within this book of traditional businesses taking new ideas on board, of young ambitious folk finding ways to carve out a rewarding living in a county where the standard career paths aren't plentiful, and of people bringing new ideas to this place where dreams really do become reality.

Grants and funding, often maligned and rarely acknowledged, have played a big part. They have been a carrot that has given the quality a boost and encouraged people to work together, unearthing Cornwall's collective strength.

Cornwall undoubtedly now produces some of the finest food and drink in the world and is home to chefs and artisans who do some amazing things with those raw materials. This book is a celebration of every one of the hard-working people who make that happen – day in, day out. Farmers and fishermen, butchers and bakers, cider-makers and cheese-makers, chefs and shopkeepers. The list is long, but common to all of them is an unerring belief in what they do. I feel privileged and proud to have worked amongst them.

On these pages we can't possibly pay homage individually to all those who are part of that picture. So we've opted for a balance between some of the time-honoured names and places you will expect to see and some newer gems we'd like you to discover. Dip in, take a culinary journey through Cornwall, find out why it has become a haven for foodlovers, and use the recipes and tips to recreate your own flavour of Cornwall.

Ruth Huxley

Ruth Huxley
Founder and Director of Cornwall Food & Drink

SEA AND SHORE

THREE FISHERS WENT SAILING
AWAY TO THE WEST, AWAY TO THE
WEST AS THE SUN WENT DOWN.
EACH THOUGHT ON THE WOMAN
WHO LOVED HIM THE BEST, AND
THE CHILDREN STOOD WATCHING
THEM OUT OF THE TOWN, FOR MEN
MUST WORK, AND WOMEN MUST
WEEP, AND THERE'S LITTLE TO EARN,
AND MANY TO KEEP, THOUGH THE
HARBOUR – BAR BE MOANING.

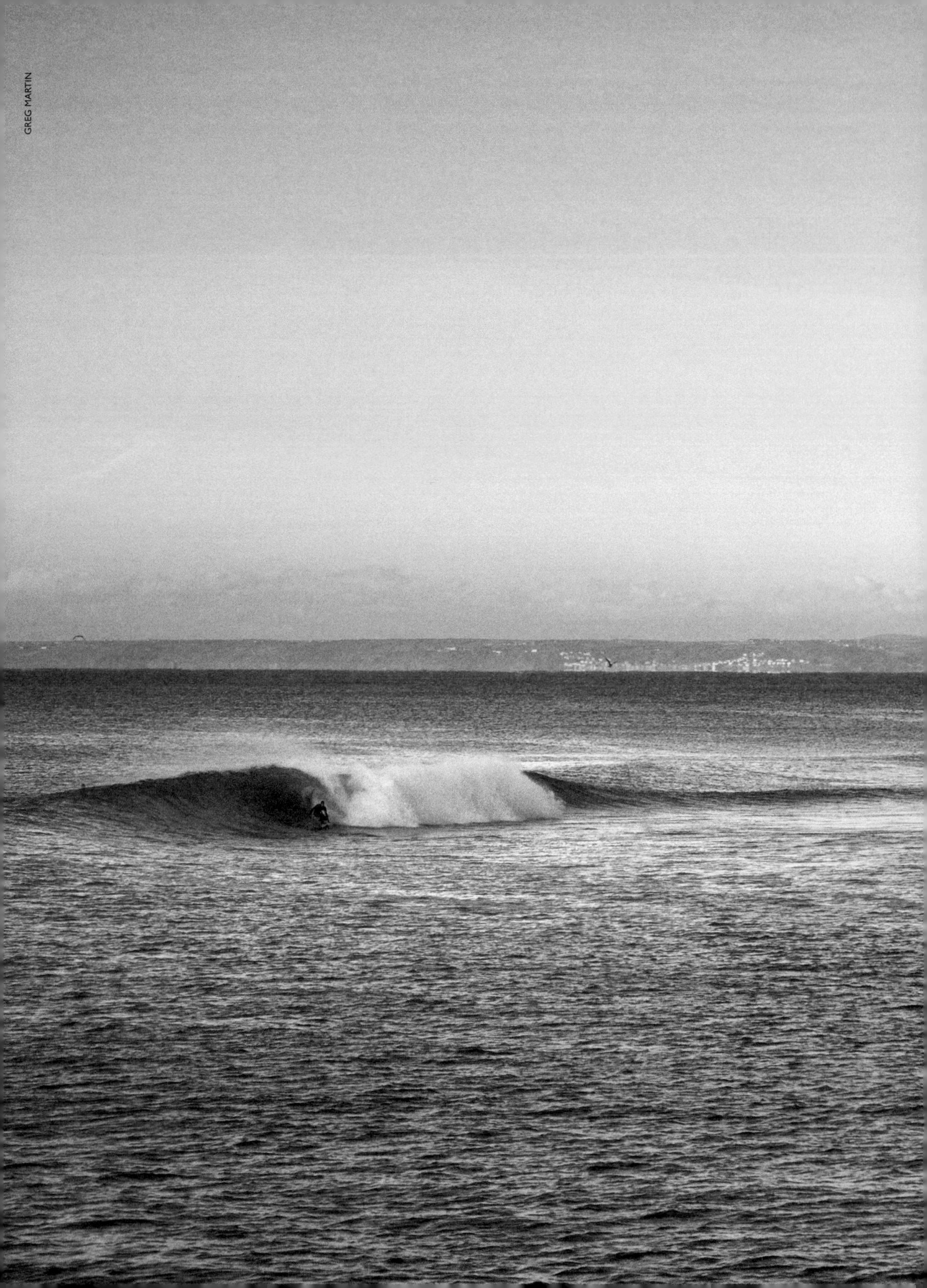
GREG MARTIN

Cornish fishermen are brave, strong souls of dry wit, weathered skin and long deep gaze, born from enduring the wrath of the Western Approaches as they compete for the rich pickings off the Cornish coast.

Most are doing what they have grown up with – what their fathers and grandfathers did and what they hope their sons and grandsons will do. Fishing is their life and the pubs and ports of Cornwall echo with their tales of courage, fortune and disaster from the unforgiving sea that is their friend and foe.

But why does anyone do one of the most dangerous jobs known to man? Like Cornish farmers, Cornish fishermen will tell you that it's not just because it's what they know; there's something about working at the mercy of nature that can be as inspirational and rewarding as it is challenging. And of course, there's always the mystery of not knowing quite what the next catch might bring.

Take a stroll around any Cornish harbour and you'll see countless small fishing boats bobbing about. These are the inshore day boats that fish the Cornish

waters using net, line and pot to catch crab, lobster, sardines, mackerel, bass and many more sought-after species. This is time-honoured fishing – and it's about as sustainable as it gets.

Cornish fishing in the 21st century is a real jewel in the county's food crown. As many as forty species can be landed on any one day from the combined fleet of day boats and larger vessels. Ironically, the fishloving people of countries such as Spain, Italy and France have always been much more eager to get their hands on Cornish fish than those closer to home and at one time nearly all the fish landed here was exported.

Thanks to the resourcefulness of the merchants and fishermen, the influence of great seafood chefs like Rick Stein and Nathan Outlaw and the advent of new ways of selling and transporting fish, this is changing. People are being tempted into trying the excellent varieties that are caught in abundance here but were not previously well known - gurnard, red mullet, megrim sole and many more – and can now buy online from the fishermen or merchants and have the freshest fish delivered directly to their door.

HEVA, HEVA!

"THROUGH STREET AND COURT WE 'HEVA' HEAR,
AND MAN THE BOATS, FOR FISH ARE NEAR;
IT NERVES OUR ARM AND SPEEDS OUR TREAD,
FOR FISH TO US ARE MEAT AND BREAD."
PERCY R. CRAFT

The Huer's cry: Before the advent of modern electronics, pilchard boats were guided to the shoals by lookouts on the cliff tops. These men, known as Huers, had a distinct call: "Heva, heva", to attract the attention of the boats and then point them to the shoals.

For centuries, pilchards were caught in abundance all around Cornwall's coast and the many 'Pilchard Palaces' were hives of industry - salting, pressing and packing the silver treasure in wooden boxes and barrels. The vast majority were shipped overseas, mainly to Italy, to be used as a tasty and nutritious way of perking up pasta, pizza and polenta. However in the 1950s the pilchard fell out of favour and by the end of the 20th century, the market had all but disappeared.

Cue Nick Howell, owner of Newlyn's Pilchard Works, who in 1998 hit upon the idea of simply dropping the word pilchard and using the more fashionable name 'Cornish sardine' (sardines and pilchards are in fact both the same fish). It worked - M&S took the bait and helped rekindle interest in the fresh, unsalted fish. By the following year grilled Cornish sardines were the talk of the town and appeared on fish counters, restaurant menus and barbecue griddles up and down the country, securing the future of Cornwall's historic sardine fishery.

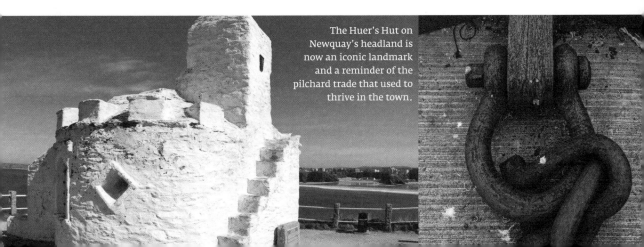

The Huer's Hut on Newquay's headland is now an iconic landmark and a reminder of the pilchard trade that used to thrive in the town.

CORNISH SARDINES

TODAY SARDINE FISHING USES THE SAME RING NET METHODS THAT HAVE BEEN USED FOR GENERATIONS. MUCH OF THE FISHING IS DONE AT THE END OF THE DAY AS DUSK ARRIVES, AND EVEN INTO THE NIGHT. AS THE SUN FADES, THE FISH RISE CLOSER TO THE SURFACE OF THE WATER AND ARE EASIER TO CATCH.

Paul Ripley is one of the UK's finest seafood chefs, but is just as happy cooking simple and inexpensive fish like sardines and mackerel as some of the more luxury varieties. We asked him why Cornish sardines are so good and what to look out for when buying and cooking them:

• Fresh sardines should have a good blue-purple sheen to their backs and be firm to the touch.

• Avoid any with split bellies and red heads as they will be old fish.

• Ask your fishmonger to scale and fillet the fish, removing any pin bones from the larger fish. Larger fish should also be gutted before cooking.

• Sardines are a very good source of omega-3 fatty acids. Much of the oil is held in the skin that crisps up beautifully when grilled.

• This makes them a great summer BBQ fish - just a good squeeze of lemon is all they will need.

• For the more adventurous, try curing or pickling them.

BECAUSE OF THEIR SIZE, SARDINES ARE PERFECT FOR LIGHT, TAPAS-STYLE DISHES SUCH AS THIS ONE OF PAUL'S

GRILLED OREGANO AND PAPRIKA STUFFED SARDINES

SERVES 8

• 16 small sardines
• Olive oil
• 3 shallots thinly sliced
• 20g breadcrumbs made from day old stale bread
• Finely grated zest of 1 lemon
• 1 tsp smoked Spanish paprika
• 1 tbsp oregano leaves
• Cornish sea salt
• Crusty bread and lemon wedges to serve

1 Heat 2 tablespoons of olive oil in a frying pan, add shallots and cook over a low heat for 5 minutes until soft. Increase the heat and add the oregano and breadcrumbs and cook for 5 minutes or until the breadcrumbs are nice and golden. Add the lemon zest and paprika and season with sea salt. Leave to cool.

2 Place 1 teaspoon of your cooled stuffing mixture into the belly cavity of the fish. Place on a well oiled tray and scatter with any remaining stuffing mixture. Drizzle with olive oil and place under the grill for 5-7 minutes until just cooked through.

3 Serve sardines at room temperature with crusty bread and lemon wedges.

'The Greeting' by Walter Langley

Newlyn's reputation for both fishing and art is celebrated on tins of sardines decorated with traditional Newlyn School of Art paintings.

CURING FISH – BEN TUNNICLIFFE

BEN IS ONE OF CORNWALL'S MOST ACCLAIMED CHEFS, NOW RUNNING THE TOLCARNE INN, A PUB THAT SERVES EXCEPTIONAL FOOD AND WINE IN A RELAXED FASHION. LOCATED JUST AROUND THE CORNER FROM NEWLYN HARBOUR, HE CAN SEE WHAT'S LANDED AND THE FISH WILL BE ON THE MENU THAT DAY.

Almost lost with the dawn of modern preservation methods such as refrigeration and canning, curing is making a comeback — and in a big way. Restaurants and chefs everywhere are touting cured meats, house-smoked specialties and homemade sausages. And, increasingly, cured fish.

Curing fish takes very little active time; days rather than the weeks it might take to cure other meats. In the case of ceviche, where fish is 'cooked' in lime juice, it's done in minutes. And since curing requires no special equipment, it's very easily done at home.

The process is simple: combine salt, sugar and/or smoke to gently draw moisture from a food to preserve it. Although almost any fish can be cured, it must be very fresh and of the best quality. Curing will not make a bad fish better or safer to eat.

Cod or pollock can be lightly cured before cooking to get some interesting flavour into the piece of fish, for example juniper and bay leaf. In this case the cure is only put on for 10-20 minutes, depending on the thickness of the fish, and thoroughly washed off before cooking. Try loose leafed tea, herbs and spices but be careful not to use anything with a really strong flavour that might totally take away the natural flavour of the fish.

The basic recipe when curing salmon, say for gravadlax, or for fish that will later be smoked is 42g of table salt and 42g of sugar per 440g of fish flesh.

"I'm surrounded by amazing producers with real passion about what they do. They're right on my doorstep so I get first pick."

BEN'S TOP TIPS

• Play around with different fish to see how they respond to curing. Some of Ben's successes are mackerel gravadlax, lavender-cured halibut, vanilla-cured sea trout (see recipe) and ceviche of sea bass.
• When cooking cured fish, try leaving the fish a little less cooked, which makes for an extra-moist piece that flakes into large, luscious chunks.
• Keep the fish refrigerated at all times, even after it is cured. Home curing works to denature the protein in the fish, in essence cooking it, but can't be counted on to render it safe to leave at room temperature.

VANILLA CURED SEA TROUT WITH LEMON VANILLA DRESSING

BEN TUNNICLIFFE TAKES US THROUGH THE PROCESS OF FISH CURING.

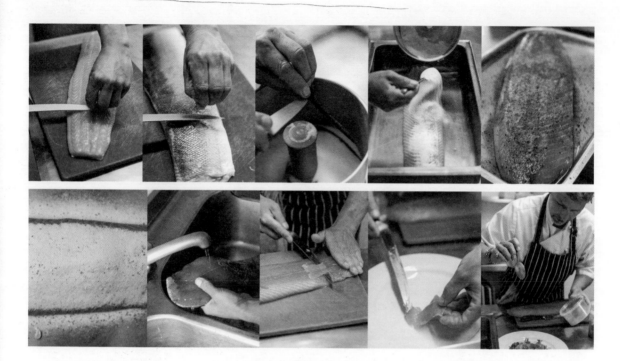

SERVES 8-12 AS A STARTER
Once cured, this will keep for a few days in the fridge, assuming you don't finish it at the first sitting.

- 1 fillet of sea trout weighing about 800g – 1kg
- 85g table salt
- 85g caster sugar
- 1 vanilla pod

LEMON VANILLA DRESSING:
- 2 lemons
- 1 tbsp sugar
- 1 vanilla pod
- White wine or cider vinegar
- Olive oil
- Salt and pepper

1 Start by trimming the fillet of sea trout of any belly to neaten up. This trim can be poached and used in some fishcakes or fish pie.

2 Turn the fish over so that the skin is uppermost. Using the point of a sharp knife remove three little circles of skin about the size of a 10p piece, taking care not to remove too much flesh. This ensures that the cure and its flavour will permeate as much of the fish as possible.

3 Now put the salt, sugar and the roughly chopped vanilla pod into a blender and blitz to get the vanilla flavour into the salt and sugar cure.

4 Take a large baking dish to catch any juices. Spoon a little of the cure into the dish and lay the sea trout fillet skin side down on this and then cover the flesh with the rest of the cure. Put more of the cure at the fat end of the fillet and less at the thin tail end to avoid over-curing.

5 Wrap the whole thing in cling film and refrigerate for 36 hours. At the end of this time it should feel firm to the touch.

6 Remove cling film, wash the fish thoroughly under cold water and pat dry. The fish is now ready to be thinly sliced and enjoyed.

7 To make the dressing squeeze the juice of the lemons into a pan, add a tablespoon of sugar and the seeds of a vanilla pod. Boil to reduce to a syrup.

8 Allow to cool slightly before adding a splash of the vinegar, some salt and pepper and approximately 3-4 times the lemon syrup's volume in olive oil. Whisk to emulsify and away you go.

THE RICK FACTOR

THE MAN WHO MADE THE WORDS CORNWALL AND FISH SYNONYMOUS AROUND THE GLOBE IS, OF COURSE, RICK STEIN AND, FOR MANY PEOPLE, A TRIP TO CORNWALL MUST INCLUDE A VISIT TO ONE OF HIS RESTAURANTS, SHOPS OR CAFÉS IN PADSTOW OR FALMOUTH.

COURTESY THE SEAFOOD RESTAURANT

Something that isn't as well known is the much wider impact Rick Stein has had on Cornwall's culinary reputation - as a breeding ground for talent. You'll find head chefs all over the county, and others who now own their own restaurants, who have worked in Rick's kitchens gaining the confidence and experience that has helped set them up in their careers. While encouraging people watching his TV shows not to be afraid of fish, Rick's influence has improved chefs' understanding of fish and seafood and helped put it on the menus of virtually every self-respecting restaurant in Cornwall – in spades.

One man who acknowledges that he wouldn't be at the giddy two Michelin starred heights he enjoys today without Rick Stein is Cornwall's

INGRID KING /VISIT CORNWALL

current champion chef, Nathan Outlaw. The story goes that a 19 year old Nathan passed a London bookseller's one evening and spotted a display in the window featuring one of Rick's books. The next day he picked up the phone and asked for a job. The guy he spoke to was Rick's head chef at the time, Paul Ripley, who suggested Nathan got himself down to Cornwall for a chat. Rick hired Nathan and he's never looked back.

Both Nathan and Paul subsequently moved on to set up their own businesses and both have since earned Michelin star status. The pair have always been on the same page about food and are currently back working together at Nathan's restaurants at the St Enodoc Hotel in Rock, just a hop across the Camel estuary from the place they first met.

From their early days under Rick Stein, a love affair with fish has dominated both men's cooking and, like so many other Cornish chefs, they will both say there's no better place to cook fish than Cornwall because the ingredients on their doorstep are simply the best in the world.

Success breeds success, and one characteristic you will find everywhere in Cornwall is a willingness to share things around, to keep the virtuous circle turning. It's therefore befitting that Nathan Outlaw, now not an unfamiliar sight on the TV screen himself, has put his name to an Academy where top college students get the chance to learn from him personally. Not just for chefs, Academy Nathan Outlaw teaches the all-important service skills too.

RICK STEIN'S FILLETS OF MEGRIM SOLE WITH SALSA VERDE MAYONNAISE

SERVES 4
- 1 loaf of slightly stale bread
- 50g plain flour
- 2 large eggs, beaten
- Vegetable oil for deep-frying
- 12 megrim sole fillets, about 65g each, skinned
- Lemon wedges, for garnish

SALSA VERDE MAYONNAISE:
- 3 tbsp chopped fresh parsley
- 1 tbsp chopped fresh mint
- 3 tbsp capers
- 6 anchovy fillets
- 1 garlic clove, crushed
- 1 tsp Dijon mustard
- 1 tbsp fresh lemon juice
- ½ tsp salt
- 6 tbsp mayonnaise

1 For the salsa verde mayonnaise, put the first seven ingredients into a pestle and mortar or food processor and grind to a coarse paste. Stir into the mayonnaise, adding more salt if required, and set aside.

2 Break the bread into small pieces. Place in a food processor and process into crumbs – they do not need to be too fine – then turn out on to a large plate. Spoon the flour on to another plate and pour the beaten eggs into a shallow dish.

3 Heat the oil for deep-frying to 190°C or until a cube of bread browns in 30 seconds. Preheat the oven to 150°C. Line a large baking sheet with paper towels.

4 Season the megrim sole fillets with a little salt and pepper. Dip the fillets into the flour, then into the beaten egg and then the bread-crumbs, pressing them on well to give an even coating.

5 Deep-fry, two pieces at a time, for 2 minutes or until crisp and golden. Remove to the baking sheet and keep hot in the oven while you cook the rest. Serve at once, with the salsa verde mayonnaise and lemon wedges.

HOW TO FILLET A FLAT FISH
WITH MARK PUCKEY OF PADSTOW SEAFOOD SCHOOL

Megrim sole, perhaps not as pretty as its Dover and Lemon counterparts, is nonetheless extremely tasty and very good value. It is sustainably fished and is in plentiful supply off the Cornish coast for most of the year, but the UK has only recently cottoned on to it.

Mark Puckey, head chef lecturer at Padstow Seafood School, uses this delectable fish to unravel one of the mysteries of food prep that few people ever attempt at home – filleting a flat fish.

1 Cut around the back of the head, down to the backbone using a sharp, thin-bladed, flexible knife. Then make a cut down the centre of the fish, from head to tail.
2 Starting at the head, slide the knife under one fillet and carefully cut it away, keeping the blade as flat and as close to the bones as possible. Remove the adjacent fillet, then turn the fish over and repeat.
3 Lay the fillet skin-side down, with the narrowest end facing you. Hold the tip of the skin with your fingers, angling the blade of the knife down towards the skin and working it away from you, start to cut between the flesh and the skin. Firmly take hold of the skin and continue to work away from you, sawing the knife from side to side, keeping the blade close against the skin until the fillet is released.
4 Trim the frills away from the edge of the skinless fillet to give it a neat finish.

BORN TO BE A SHELLFISHERMAN

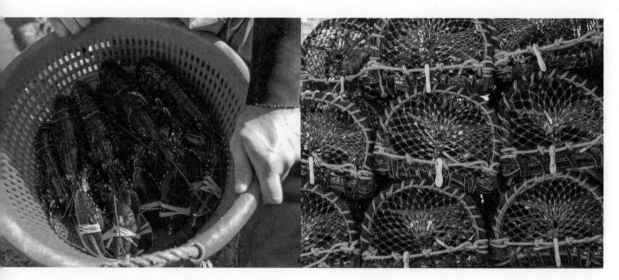

The love of fishing runs deep through Jeremy Hosking's blood - it's in his DNA. His family have been braving the Cornish seas off Porthleven and Penzance for over 100 years. At one time there were as many as 20 crabbers fishing out of Porthleven. Their names "Wispering Hope" (sic), "Boy Bob", "Boy Frank", "Provider", "Girl Joan", "Reliance", "Morning Star" reflect their importance to the owners and are a haunting reminder of crews gone by. This started to change in the 1920s when boats were sold and families disappeared from the trade. Then in the '50s Porthleven's fish market closed and the trade transferred to Newlyn.

The Hosking family are one of those who have stuck it out through thick and thin. So it was no surprise that as a young man Jeremy, known now simply as The Shellfisherman, didn't have to make a career choice - the sea had chosen him already. He left school on a Friday and went to sea the following Monday and has been fishing ever since.

Nowadays he catches only lobster and crab but it's no easier than it was for the generations before him. A fisherman's livelihood is still dependent on the weather.

Some days the boats can't sail, and even when they do there is no guarantee of a catch. A long cold winter like the ones we've had in recent years can be hard because the fish stay in hibernation.

As the tide ebbs and flows so do the fishermen's lives. Lives ruled by the sea. Filled with sunrises, sunsets and sea spray. It is, by any standard, a life less than ordinary.

A DAY IN THE LIFE

- A shellfisherman sets off around 5-6am.
- Once in the fishing grounds the pots are hauled in and the catch checked (strict rules ensure the sustainability of shellfishing and some such as undersize or egg-bearing stock must be put back).
- Each pot needs to be rebaited and dropped by 3pm in order to make it back to Newlyn by 5pm – if they miss the market they can't sell the catch.

The sea bed condition and what they feed on mean that Cornish shellfish have a great flavour and are in high demand"

THE PERFECT CRAB SANDWICH

IT'S THE STUFF OF SEASIDE HOLIDAYS. MAYBE IT'S THE SALT IN THE AIR, OR JUICY CRAB AS FRESH AS IT GETS, BUT A CRAB SANDWICH ALWAYS TASTES BETTER BESIDE THE SEA.

Stuart McGuire, chef at The Rum and Crab Shack overlooking the harbour at the classic seaside town of St Ives, shares his tips for making the perfect crab sandwich.

1 Steam a good size spider crab for about 8-10 minutes or boil it for 10 minutes.
2 Pick the crab (see below) while it's still warm and separate the brown meat from the white.
3 Flake up the white meat with a fork.
4 Pass the brown meat through a coarse sieve.
5 Add to the white meat: chopped parsley (and chopped wild garlic when in season), lemon juice, good olive oil, Cornish sea salt and cracked black pepper.
6 Spread unsalted Cornish butter on two slices of fresh granary bread* then paste the brown meat on both buttered sides.
7 Fill generously with the white meat mixture, cut into quarters and present with extra lemon wedges. Watch it disappear!

*If you're feeling adventurous, home made onion, herb and horseradish bread is great with this: one part white flour to two parts malt flour plus diced onion, herbs and freshly grated horseradish, all sweated in olive oil.

TOP TIP
Purists never put mayo in a crab sandwich.

HOW TO PICK A SPIDER CRAB

1 Twist the claws and legs off your cooked spider crab.
2 Hold the crab upside down with head forwards. Using your thumbs lift off the back, away from you, as if you were opening the lid of a box.
3 Pick out the 'Dead Man's Fingers' and discard. These are the grey spongy gills. It's a common misconception that they are poisonous, but they don't make good eating.

4 Cut the body into quarters with a large knife and, using a lobster pick or teaspoon, pick out the meat.
5 Keep the brown meat separate - it can be quite runny. Crabs vary.
6 Break each claw in half, then crack open with the back of a large knife. Use nut crackers to crack open near the pincers, and again pull meat from the carcass. Repeat for the legs.

Easily identified, the spider crab is highly sought after for its meat, and can grow to a large size, the shell up to eight inches across. Often shunned because it can be fiddly, anyone who makes the effort will be well rewarded with the sweetest, most succulent meat.

WIZARD OF THE WEST

SCALLOPS ARE ANOTHER CORNISH
SEAFOOD DELIGHT. NATHAN
OUTLAW SHARES A RECIPE THAT
CALLS FOR THE FRESHEST, PLUMPEST,
JUICIEST CORNISH SCALLOPS. THIS
WOULD BE EQUALLY GOOD AS A
DINNER PARTY STARTER OR LAZY
LUNCH. THE PICKLED BEETROOT
AND APPLE WORK REALLY WELL
WITH THE SWEET FRESH SCALLOP
AND SALTY BACON.

DAVID LOFTUS

SCALLOP TARTARE WITH PICKLED BEETROOT, BACON AND APPLE

SERVES 4

- 300g scallops, cleaned and corals removed
- 4 rashers of smoked streaky bacon
- 1 apple
- 1 shallot, peeled and finely chopped
- 2 tsp chopped gherkin
- 2 tsp finely chopped chives
- Cornish sea salt and freshly ground black pepper

PICKLED BEETROOT:

- 200g raw beetroot
- 2 tsp red wine vinegar
- 3 tsp sherry vinegar
- 1 shallot, peeled and finely chopped
- 1 garlic clove, peeled and finely chopped
- 1 tsp chopped thyme
- 4 tbsp olive oil

TO ASSEMBLE AND SERVE:

- ½ quantity mayonnaise (see opposite)
- 4 slices of sourdough bread
- Handful of rocket leaves
- Lemon wedges

1 First prepare the pickled beetroot. Put the beetroot in a saucepan, pour on water to cover and add the wine vinegar. Bring to a simmer, add a pinch of salt and cook for 25 minutes. Leave the beetroot to cool in the water until you are able to handle it, then remove and peel off the skin. Cut the beetroot into 1cm dice, using a sharp knife. Place in a bowl with the sherry vinegar, shallot, garlic and thyme. Season with salt and pepper and drizzle with the olive oil. Mix well and then cover and leave to marinate for at least 2 hours.

2 Preheat your grill. Lay the bacon on a grill tray and grill on both sides until very crispy. Allow to cool down, then chop the bacon into small pieces.

3 On a clean board, carefully slice and dice the scallop meat into 5mm pieces.

4 Peel, quarter and core the apple, then cut into 5mm dice. Put the scallops and apple into a bowl with the shallot, gherkin, bacon and chives. Add 2 teaspoons mayonnaise and mix well. Taste for seasoning and add salt and pepper as required.

5 To serve, toast the bread on both sides and place on 4 serving plates. Spoon the scallop tartare neatly on top. Spoon some of the marinated beetroot with a little of its dressing alongside. Scatter over the rocket and serve with lemon wedges and the rest of the mayonnaise in a bowl on the side for guests to help themselves.

"I'm spoilt by the quality of ingredients I have access to here and never forget that the fishermen, farmers and producers have as much passion about what they do as I have."

THE GENTLE GIANT OF THE CORNISH FOOD WORLD, NATHAN'S OUTWARDLY THOUGHTFUL AND CALM AIR BELIES A GRITTY DETERMINATION THAT LURKS BENEATH. HE'S A MAN WHO IS CLEARLY AIMING TO BE THE BEST IN THE WORLD AT WHAT HE DOES AND, AS OWNER OF THE HIGHEST MICHELIN-RANKING SEAFOOD RESTAURANT IN THE UK, YOU MIGHT SAY HE IS ALREADY WELL ON HIS WAY!

NATHAN'S HOME MADE MAYONNAISE

Everyone thinks home made mayo is really tricky, but as long as you follow the instructions it's quick and straightforward, and tastes a million times better than a dollop from a jar. This is Nathan's standard recipe and will keep in the fridge for a couple of days:

- 3 free range egg yolks
- 1 tsp English mustard
- Juice of ½ a lemon or 2 tsps cider vinegar or white wine vinegar
- 300ml light rapeseed oil
- Cornish sea salt and freshly ground black pepper

- Put the egg yolks, mustard and lemon juice or vinegar into a bowl and whisk together for 1 minute.
- Now slowly add the oil, drop by drop to begin with, then in a steady stream, whisking continuously, until the mixture is emulsified and thick.

Alternatively, you can make the mayonnaise in a blender or food processor, blending the egg yolks, mustard and lemon juice or vinegar for 1 minute then adding the oil slowly through the funnel with the motor running.

FAL OYSTERS

A NATIVE OF THE RIVER FAL, THE OSTREA EDULIS IS A VERY SPECIAL OYSTER, UNIQUELY HARVESTED BY BOATS THAT CAREFULLY DREDGE UNDER SAIL OR OAR; NEVER POWERED BY OTHER MEANS.

THESE CELEBRATED OYSTERS ARE EASILY RECOGNISED BY THEIR ROUND SHAPE, DISTINCTLY DIFFERENT FROM THE ELONGATED SHAPE OF THE MORE COMMON FARMED OYSTERS.

The season, which runs from 1st October to 31st March, is heralded by the Falmouth Oyster Festival, which celebrates these tasty molluscs and includes a traditional race of the licensed Falmouth working boats.

Paul Wadham, head chef at the stylish Hotel Tresanton at St Mawes, just a couple of miles from where these delicacies are harvested, thinks these oysters are too special to cook and need to be eaten very simply. A squeeze of fresh lemon juice and black pepper is enough, alternatively try with this simple shallot vinaigrette:

Finely dice a shallot and mix with a really good quality wine vinegar such as a Cabernet Sauvignon. The acidity will complement the creaminess of the oyster without spoiling it.

UK
CQ 710
EC

TOP TIP
Buy Fal Oysters from a reputable supplier who will show you the health mark indicating that they have been cleaned and purified.

For most people, the greatest mystery about oysters is how to open them. Paul shows you how.

1 Lay the oyster in a folded cloth on a flat surface and firmly grasp it with the flat part of the shell facing up.

2 Push the point of a sharp knife into the hinge (pointy end) of the shell. Slide the knife from side to side to prise open the shell.

3 Run the knife along the flat 'top', twisting it slightly. Cut the muscle and lift off the top but be careful to retain the juices.

4 Remove any fragments of shell.

Shucking is an American term for getting into an oyster. The English use the expression 'cutting' or 'opening'.

GO WILD IN THE COUNTRY

WE NEED THE TONIC OF WILDNESS...
AT THE SAME TIME THAT WE ARE
EARNEST TO EXPLORE AND LEARN ALL
THINGS, WE REQUIRE THAT ALL THINGS
BE MYSTERIOUS AND UNEXPLORABLE, THAT
LAND AND SEA BE INDEFINITELY WILD,
UNSURVEYED AND UNFATHOMED BY US
BECAUSE UNFATHOMABLE. WE CAN NEVER
HAVE ENOUGH OF NATURE.

The sea is a huge part of Cornish life, but there's another whole world to discover when you step back onto dry land. From the sandy shoreline to the tops of the granite moors, from dense woodland to vast open spaces, not to mention nearly 300 miles of South West Coast Path, the Cornish countryside is ripe for exploring.

Whatever the season, whatever the weather, there is always somewhere to go, something to do and, most importantly, something good to eat and drink along the way. In the wilds of Cornwall, delightful country pubs and coastal cafés pop up out of nowhere and can be relied upon for a warm welcome and hearty fodder. These are the places that often use the tiny suppliers in their immediate vicinity – growing startlingly fresh salads and fruit just down the road, picked and on the plate the same day. When people talk of 'the supply chain', this type of partnership is every bit as important to Cornwall as those of much larger scale.

For those who prefer DIY food on a day out, the Cornish coast and countryside offer endless possibilities for perfect picnic spots or, naturally, the best beach barbie ever. Wherever you choose to venture, keep a lookout for some of Cornwall's classic 'honesty box' goodies nestling in gateways down country lanes. Freshly laid free range eggs and freshly picked fruit, veg and flowers can all be found. Just make your choice and pop your money in the box. It's a system based entirely on trust, and it works – a refreshing alternative to the high tech, high security features that surround most of our lives.

The countryside is also home to an amazing bounty of wild food, once welcomed by many families to help make ends meet, but almost forgotten about when 'convenience' became king. Now shooting, fishing and foraging are all back in vogue, but this time driven by a desire to get back to nature, re-discover the origins of food and mark the changing of the seasons. It's also healthy and sustainable and there can be few places that offer more options for going wild than Cornwall.

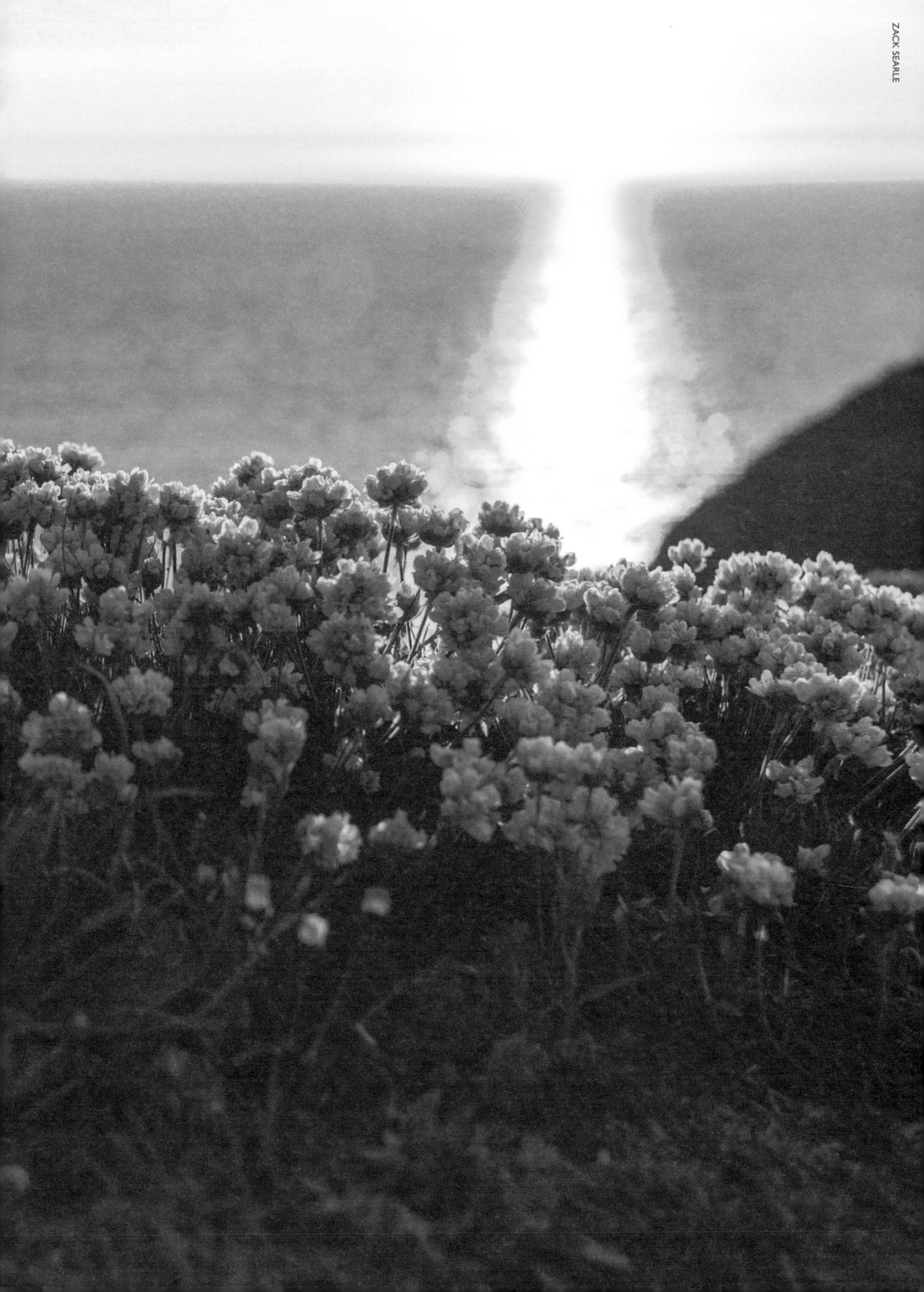
ZACK SEARLE

MOTHER NATURE'S LARDER

THE GENEROUS CORNISH HEDGEROWS AND FIELDS ARE A CORNUCOPIA OF WILD FOOD - THE SALAD SUPERMARKETS OF THE GREAT OUTDOORS. SO WITH A TREND THAT BRINGS HEDGEROW COUTURE TO OUR TABLES MAKING A COMEBACK, THE FREE LARDERS OF THE CORNISH COUNTRYSIDE OFFER RICH PICKINGS.

Once you step into the world of foraging, a little knowledge goes a long way. Some of the commonest edible plants are the easiest to recognise: sorrel, nettles, pennywort, wild garlic and three-cornered leek grow in abundance throughout the Cornish countryside and can be used in fresh salads, pesto, risottos or soups. Mushrooms are a different ball game and, with over 4,000 different types in the UK, some deadly poisonous, it's always best to stick to what you are absolutely sure about. But for everything else, a long forgotten world of traditional yet tantalising treats, from elderflower cordial to homemade jam, sloe gin to sorrel soup, awaits.

WILD FOOD FORAGING

FIONA WERE, HEAD CHEF AT THE GREENBANK HOTEL, OVERLOOKING FALMOUTH BAY, IS SOMETHING OF A FORAGING AFICIONADO. FOLLOW HER SEASONAL GUIDE TO WILD CORNWALL AND KEEP YOUR LARDER STOCKED FOR FREE.

wild garlic

Spring is an exciting time as everything awakes. The arrival of the wild garlic means it's time to get out and about because this is one of the most versatile wild ingredients. Its fresh leaves are wonderful folded through risottos or made into pesto. They are also delicious cooked like spinach to accompany spring lamb and amazing wrapped around halloumi and griddled. Three cornered leek takes over once wild garlic flowers are finished, with all parts of the plant being edible, including the flowers. Gorse flowers, hawthorn flowers and primroses are also lovely additions infused in pannacottas and of course make great wine too!

elderflower

Summer's two quintessential delights - wild strawberries and elderflowers - also make great partners. Wild strawberries are much more potent than their cultivated cousins and add concentrated flavour bursts to summer desserts: well worth the hunt, and easy to cultivate as long as you can protect them from birds. Elderflowers make an exquisitely perfumed sparkling wine or cordial. Use them to add flavour to ice creams, sorbets, cakes and other desserts.

wild strawberries

"Wild ingredients are perfect as accents to dishes, introducing interesting flavours, textures and seasonal notes."

crab apples

Autumn is the season of foraging bounty, with wild mushrooms, including the intensely flavoured and much sought after chanterelles, all manner of berries, wild plums, rosehips, nuts, leaves and crab apples in abundance. This is the time to fill your store cupboard to see you through the cold months – let your imagination run riot making sweet preserves and pickles and infusing for liqueurs and wines.

Winter signals a time for curling up by the fire and enjoying the fruits of your labours, but hardy foragers can still find sweet chestnuts, wood sorrel, watercress and a few other greens. In the last weeks of winter, hogweed shoots (an acquired taste) and nettles appear in Cornwall.

nettles

sweet chestnuts

foraging rules

A FEW POINTS TO CONSIDER BEFORE YOU RUN OFF INTO THE COUNTRY:

- Know what you're picking. If you're not confident, many professional foragers run courses.
- Ask for permission from the landowner if you intend foraging on private land.
- For obvious reasons avoid roadsides and plants at low height where dog walkers are prevalent.
- Always leave more than you take; take a little here and there, leaving enough for the wildlife to enjoy.
- Legally, you can only forage in the wild for your own personal use. So even jars of blackberry jam or elderflower cordial could come under scrutiny if sold.

TOP TIP
If you want to use foraged food for commercial purposes, try collecting seeds or cuttings to grow in your own garden, or even in pots.

CLARE'S HEDGEROW MUFFINS

Clare's Cottage Bread and Cakes is one of Cornwall's true cottage industries. Run by Clare Sivam from her cottage kitchen in the heart of the Cornish countryside, everything she makes has the exquisite quality and style of someone who puts their soul into everything they do. Use blackberries picked from the hedgerows to make these delectable muffins – they have much more flavour than the cultivated ones. Delicious served warm from the oven for breakfast/brunch or cold with afternoon tea.

MAKES 12 MUFFINS

- 255g self-raising flour
- 1½ tsp baking powder
- 170g caster sugar
- 110g Cornish unsalted butter (melted)
- 1 large free range egg
- 150ml full fat milk
- 150ml live plain yoghurt
- 1½ tsp pure vanilla extract
- 140g foraged blackberries
- 1 eating apple (peeled, cored and chopped into small chunks)
- Icing sugar for dusting
- Greaseproof paper

1 Cut twelve 15cm x 15cm greaseproof paper squares.
2 Line a muffin tin with the squares – you will need to push the papers into the tin. Don't worry if the papers don't behave, the weight of the mixture will ensure that the papers sink into the trays.
3 Preheat the oven to 180°C.
4 Sieve the flour and baking powder into a bowl.
5 Stir in the sugar.
6 Add the melted butter, egg, milk, yoghurt and vanilla.
7 Stir everything together with a fork.
8 Add the blackberries and apple. Fold in gently.
9 Plop a tablespoon of mixture into the middle of each muffin square.
10 Bake for 30 – 35 minutes until golden brown.
11 Leave to cool in the tin for 5 minutes.
12 Place on a cooling rack, sprinkle with icing sugar and enjoy!

WILD STRAWBERRY AND ELDERFLOWER FROZEN NOUGAT

BY FIONA WERE, HEAD CHEF AT THE GREENBANK HOTEL, FALMOUTH

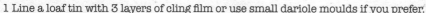

- 100g caster sugar
- 60g liquid glucose
- 150g wild flower honey
- 8 free range egg whites
- 800ml Cornish double cream
- 1 cup wild strawberries
- 100ml elderflower cordial

1 Line a loaf tin with 3 layers of cling film or use small dariole moulds if you prefer.

2 Purée the wild strawberries and elderflower cordial together. Set aside until required.

3 Place the sugar, glucose and honey into a small saucepan. Place over medium heat and stir until sugar is dissolved. Boil to 116°C on a sugar thermometer.

4 When the syrup is nearly ready, whip the egg whites to stiff peak stage. When the syrup has reached the correct temperature, carefully pour it onto the egg whites, in a steady stream, with the mixer beating all the time. Continue beating until the meringue is quite cold.

5 Whip the cream to soft peaks and then fold into the cooled meringue mix. Ripple through the wild strawberry and elderflower purée. Spoon into the prepared loaf tin or individual dariole moulds.

6 Tap gently to remove air bubbles. Place in the freezer and leave overnight to freeze.

If you have used a loaf tin, unmould the frozen nougat, remove the cling film and slice thickly to serve. Otherwise, dip the base of the dariole moulds into hot water to loosen, then shake and tip out into your hand. Accompany with more wild strawberries, shortbread and a glass of Polgoon elderflower fizz.

WELL PRESERVED

ONE OF THE MOST TRADITIONAL AND DELICIOUS WAYS OF PUTTING SEASONAL GLUTS FROM THE GARDEN OR HEDGEROW TO GOOD USE IS BY MAKING YOUR OWN JAM AND CHUTNEY. TONY AND SARAH MARSLAND OF CORNISH MEADOW PRESERVES, WHO HAVE BEEN MAKING PRESERVES BY HAND IN SMALL BATCHES SINCE 1987, SHARE SOME OF THEIR TIPS FOR PERFECT RESULTS.

- Only use sound fruit as any bruised or bad fruit will make an inferior product and affect the keeping qualities of the end product.
- Plums and berries with a skin, such as blackcurrants and blueberries (not strawberries), benefit from freezing before using for jam. It softens the cell wall and therefore reduces the cooking time.
- Always soften the fruit in a little water with lemon juice added, cooking gently before adding the sugar. If you add the sugar too soon, the skin of the fruit becomes leathery and tough.
- When making plum, apricot or damson jam you don't need to stone the fruit first. If you cook the whole fruit gently in a little water and lemon juice until soft then squash with a potato masher before adding the sugar, hey presto! The stones will rise to the surface and you can just skim them off.
- When making chutney add all the ingredients together at the beginning of the cooking except the sugar as it may inhibit the softening of the other ingredients. Cook gently and keep stirring or you will have a burnt pan and tainted chutney. Add the sugar 10 minutes before the end of cooking then let the chutney rest before potting up. During cooking the liquid tends to rise to the surface, so by letting it rest for 20 minutes it gets re-absorbed.

SHORELINE FORAGING

AS WELL AS THE FIELDS AND HEDGEROWS, CORNWALL IS SURROUNDED BY ANOTHER NATURAL LARDER ALONG ITS SHORELINE - SEAWEEDS AND LEAVES THAT MAKE FOR SOME SUPERB COOKING. SEAWEEDS ARE HIGH IN IODINE AND OTHER ESSENTIAL MINERALS AND SOME ARE SAID TO HAVE MEDICINAL BENEFITS AND EVEN BE A NATURAL SLIMMING AID. CHECK OUT THESE TIPS ON WHAT TO LOOK OUT FOR ON THE BEACH AND HOW TO EAT IT FROM ADAM CLARK, EXECUTIVE CHEF AT BEDRUTHAN STEPS HOTEL, JUST A STONE'S THROW AWAY FROM BEAUTIFUL MAWGAN PORTH BEACH.

"The wild ingredients are always exciting to find. It's part of the hunter gatherer in me that makes going out and bringing them back to the kitchen the best thing about doing this---that's when the creative side of me gets its soul fed."

BLADDERWRACK
The dark knobbly seaweed that can be found all year round but, as with all seaweeds, is better in the spring and autumn when the sea is cooler. Wash thoroughly and place in a pan of plain boiling water; watch it turn from black to bright green. Cut the lumpy bits off, and use the fronds in sauces and stews.

THONGWEED
A khaki-beige coloured seaweed that consists of long, thin and very slippery strands, quite tricky to hold on to. Boil like bladderwrack to remove some of its stickiness and chop up the now bright green strands to add a distinctively prawny flavour to stir-fries.

LAVER
Found particularly on the rocks of Constantine Bay and Booby's Bay on the North Cornwall coast. Wash well and boil for four hours until you are left with a pulp. Great for making the traditional Welsh laverbread – coat little patties of the pulp in breadcrumbs and shallow fry.

OARWEED
A long strand seaweed found at deep tide (sometimes requires paddling to collect). Wash, then dry and snip into squares. Deep fry for under 20 seconds to make fantastic crisps. Used in Japan and China to make a soup stock and is also used as a thickener.

SEA PURSLANE
The young leaves are best in May and can be found in the salt marshes in tidal areas – the Gannel in Newquay is the perfect place to find it. Eat it raw and throw it on salads for garnish. It tastes a little like peas.

MARSH SAMPHIRE
June is the month for marsh samphire when the asparagus-like, salty, bright green spears poke up through the ground. Boil or steam to remove some of the saltiness but retain its bite. Great with fish and risotto.

ROCK SAMPHIRE
Much rarer than marsh samphire, the stems and leaves look a bit like reindeer antlers. Rock samphire has a strong, somewhat acquired taste but is good pickled in a cider vinegar and eaten with oysters or as a relish for other seafood.

SEA BEETS
The spinach of the sea but much more robust, it is the ancient relative of beetroot and chard and its leaves look very similar. Look for it at tidelines and in saltmarshes. Wilt and use under fish or in quiches and pancakes for delicious flavour.

COASTLINE FORAGING

THE MILES AND MILES OF CORNISH COASTAL PATHS AREN'T ONLY GREAT FOR WALKING, THEY OFFER A UNIQUE COLLECTION OF HARDY PLANTS AND FLOWERS THAT CAN BE USED IN COOKING TOO. HERE'S ADAM'S LUSCIOUS GORSE-INSPIRED RECIPE.

CORNISH COASTLINE GORSEFLOWER FUDGE

- 450g caster sugar
- 22½g golden syrup
- 150g unsalted Cornish butter
- 75ml Cornish double cream
- 75ml the thick part of coconut milk
- A good handful of picked over gorseflower petals

1 Put all ingredients EXCEPT the gorseflower petals in a heavy based, tall sided saucepan.
2 Heat gently stirring all the time, making sure all the sugar has dissolved completely.
3 When it feels like everything has come together and you are sure the sugar has dissolved, stop stirring, turn up the heat and put a sugar thermometer into the pan.
4 Boil until it reaches soft ball stage (120°C); this could happen quite fast so watch the thermometer carefully.
5 Once 120°C is reached remove pan from heat and leave to stand for 10 minutes.
6 During this time, lightly grease a suitable tray or container and line with cling film or greaseproof kitchen paper.
7 Next beat vigorously until the mixture thickens and stir through the gorseflower petals. Be patient as it may take some beating but you need the mixture to become a bit grainy and come away from the base of the pan.
8 Pour the fudge into the container.
9 Leave for at least three hours to firm up. Remove from the container, cut into small squares and store in an airtight box or tin.

EVERYTHING YOU DIDN'T KNOW ABOUT CORNISH GORSE

- Gorse flowers have a strong coconut aroma and fruity pineapple taste.
- Eat the flowers raw in a salad for taste and colour, infuse in boiling water to make a tea or brew up a full-bodied, coconut flavoured wine.
- Be prepared – gorse flowers have hefty spikes, wear leather gardening gloves and heavy clothing to protect you.
- High in protein, gorse is excellent fodder for moorland ponies and cattle.

Also look out for:

- Wild Rose: found here and there on the sand dunes, the petals have a flavour reminiscent of Turkish delight. Great in jam or infused in milk for ice cream.
- Alexanders: looks a little like parsley and has a very distinct flavour - a bit too strong raw, but steaming the stems for 10 minutes leaves a delicate taste, reminiscent of angelica. Great with seafood, or perhaps candied. Fab folded into a veggie curry.

GAME ON

Mention game to the man or woman on the street and you're sure to get a mixed reaction. Many people have never tried it, don't know what to do with it, or are confused about the shooting bit. As such, this source of nutritious, lean, inexpensive and sustainable meat is vastly under-used.

It may seem odd, but conservation and shooting in fact go hand-in-hand - healthy birds and deer generally don't exist without good management, and that means controlling the numbers. Unchecked, deer, rabbits and other game are prolific breeders that cause major damage to crops and countryside.

Perhaps the biggest challenge is what to do with the meat once you've bagged it. The easy option is to purchase game fully prepped from a game specialist or reputable local butcher. Many Cornish butchers carry rabbit, pheasant and venison, according to the season. However, dealing with it straight from the field isn't as tricky as you might think.

Here's Cornish game specialist Chris Perkins' way of dealing with pheasant:

- Crown it – put your thumb at the pointed end of the breast and peel it back, taking the breast off the backbone but keeping it on the breastbone. This way you don't even need to gut it, but the flip side is that you don't get any crispy skin.
- Overcome this by covering the breast with bacon to give some extra flavour. The fat also helps prevent it drying out as it cooks.
- Put in the oven at 170°C for no more than 30 minutes, frequently basting the meat.

RAGOÛT OF CORNISH GAME BIRDS

Ken Symons runs Oliver's, one of Falmouth's top spots for great food, and loves cooking with game. This game stew is made using game birds that are partly-cooked and finished off in a rich sauce made of their own bones. It is exactly the sort of food that would have been eaten by Chaucer, at the court of Henry IV.

SERVES 4

- A selection of Cornish game birds such as pheasant, partridge, woodcock
- 50g Cornish butter
- 3 chopped shallots
- 1 carrot, diced
- 1 stick of celery, finely sliced
- 1 tbsp plain flour
- A bouquet garni of orange peel strips
- 150ml red or white wine
- 100g sliced mushrooms
- Salt, pepper, cayenne pepper and a little lemon juice to season
- Orange wedges and fried bread croutons to serve

STOCK:

- 1 carrot
- Celery stick
- A handful of tomatoes
- 1 onion
- 2 cloves garlic
- Bay leaf and sprigs of rosemary and thyme
- 6 whole black peppercorns
- 1 glass of red or white wine
- 1- 1¼ l water
- 2 tbsp oil

1. Roast your game birds rare. Cut the meat from the carcasses into neat cubes. Keep the carcasses.
2. To make the stock, chop all the vegetables roughly, then brown them in a saucepan with the oil.
3. Add the wine, then add the chopped carcasses along with the herbs and spices.
4. Add the water and cook, uncovered, on a very low heat for two hours.
5. Pass the stock through a sieve and season to taste with salt and pepper.
6. To make the ragoût, fry the mushrooms in a little butter and season with salt, pepper and lemon juice.
7. Melt the remaining butter in a saucepan and cook the shallots until soft and golden, before adding the carrot and celery. Now add the flour (try using browned flour for a richer stew: roast the flour in the oven for 40 minutes at 140°C then sieve it) and whisk in your stock a third at a time to prevent lumps forming.
8. Add the bouquet garni and simmer for 20 minutes to make a thick sauce. Remove the bouquet garni, add the wine, mushrooms and diced game and simmer very gently for a further 10 minutes. Add a little cayenne pepper to season.
9. Serve in bowls with orange wedges and fried bread croutons.

THE SEASON

Strict rules govern the shooting and taking of game. For starters, it's essential to respect the open and close seasons to protect breeding patterns, and it's more complicated than you might think as the seasons vary from place to place.

GAME SEASONS IN CORNWALL

Type of game	Open season
Woodcock	1st Oct – 31st Jan
Pheasant	1st Oct – 1st Feb
Partridge	1st Sep – 1st Feb
Red Deer	
Stag	1st Aug – 30th Apr
Hind	1st Nov – 31st Mar
Fallow deer	
Buck	1st Aug – 30th Apr
Doe	1st Nov – 31st Mar
Roe deer	
Buck	1st Apr – 31st Oct
Doe	1st Nov – 31st Mar

ROASTED VENISON LOIN – CAULIFLOWER PURÉE – RED WINE & DAMSON JUS

BEN PRIOR, CHEF PROPRIETOR OF BEN'S CORNISH KITCHEN AT MARAZION, IS ONE OF CORNWALL'S YOUNG, TALENTED AND AMBITIOUS CHEFS. WE ASKED HIM TO LIFT THE LID ON HIS FAVOURITE VENISON DISH.

SERVES 4

- 4 x 200g pieces of trimmed venison loin
- 50g dried cep mushrooms, powdered
- 50g Cornish butter
- 2 tbsp cold pressed rapeseed oil

RED WINE SAUCE:

- 300ml beef or veal stock
- 110ml red wine
- 2 tbsp damson jam, or try Cornish Kea plum jam
- 50g Cornish butter

CAULIFLOWER PURÉE:

- 1 large cauliflower, cut into florets
- 50g Cornish butter
- 110ml Cornish double cream

1 Remove the venison from the fridge, dust all over with mushroom powder and leave to sit for 20 minutes.

2 Warm the butter and oil in an ovenproof pan, lightly brown off the meat, then roast at 190°C for 12 minutes.

3 Take out of the oven and rest for 10 minutes while finishing the other jobs.

4 Place the stock into a saucepan, bring to the boil, then turn down the heat and simmer for 5-7 minutes until the liquid has reduced by two thirds.

5 Add the red wine and repeat, cooking until the liquid has reduced by two thirds then add the jam and stir until it is mixed in.

6 Add the butter, season to taste with salt and freshly ground black pepper, and whisk until the sauce is glossy.

7 Cook the cauliflower florets in boiling water for 4-5 minutes, or until just tender, and drain.

8 Blend to a purée with the butter and cream in a food processor. Season with salt and freshly ground black pepper.

9 To serve, place the venison on a bed of the cauliflower purée; gently pour over the sauce. Really good with gnocchi and a colourful vegetable such as rainbow chard.

A TASTE OF SUMMER

PICNICS ARE ALL ABOUT RELAXING, ENJOYING GOOD FOOD WITH GREAT COMPANY IN FANTASTIC LOCATIONS. PICNICS PUT TOGETHER ON IMPULSE CAN BE THE MOST FUN AND EMMA DOUGLAS, OWNER OF PICNIC CORNWALL, A FAB DELI AND CAFÉ IN FALMOUTH, SHARES HER TIPS FOR THINGS TO KEEP IN THE STORE CUPBOARD AND FRIDGE SO YOU CAN BE READY IN A FLASH NEXT TIME THE SUN SHINES.

- Sliced salamis and ham, such as Deli Farm – easy to eat, good keepers and truly delicious.
- At least two different cheeses - perhaps a wedge of Cornish Blue and a creamy Cornish camembert.
- A couple of choices of good chutney - to serve straight from the jar.
- Cornish rapeseed or chilli oil - for dipping bread.
- Cornish spring water, elderflower pressé or pressed apple juice - perfect thirst quenchers.
- Cornish blush cider or rosé wine - for added relaxation if you need it.

Last minute additions to pick up from your local deli:
- Crusty baguette to tear and share.
- A few salady bits and bobs.
- Fresh fruit and Cornish clotted cream to finish.
(Alternatively, call ahead and let them put the whole lot together for you).

PORT ELIOT HOUSE AND GARDEN, ST GERMANS
Port Eliot is an ancient gem and a stunning Grade 1 listed house with beautiful gardens and woodlands. You can get lost amongst the rhododendrons and camellias, or walk by the estuary. Take a leisurely picnic by the river and you will be able to see why Port Eliot has been voted the best UK picnic spot in the Hudson's Heritage Awards.

THE PERFECT PICNIC SPOT

There are thousands of wonderful places to enjoy a picnic in Cornwall. Part of the fun is finding your own special places, but here are four that won't disappoint.

POLLYJOKE, CUBERT

A short walk from Cubert Common along a sandy path and down to Pollyjoke beach will work up an appetite for a beach picnic at this off the beaten track picnic destination.

KYNANCE COVE, LIZARD

Voted one of the best picnic spots along the entirety of the South West Coast Path, Kynance Cove is a beautiful, tropical-esque cove down on the Lizard peninsula. A picnic spot for romance, pack fizz and strawberries to make it special.

POLPERRO, SOUTH EAST CORNWALL

A picture perfect Cornish fishing village with spectacular views. Winding streets, and tiny cottages perched on steep slopes overlooking the harbour make this one of the prettiest villages in Cornwall. Climb up out of the harbour to find the perfect picnic spot and watch the fishing boats chug home with their day's catch.

SWELLPHOTOGRAPHY/SHUTTERSTOCK

PETER CADE/VISIT CORNWALL

WOODLAND WONDERLAND

FULL TO THE BRIM WITH WILDLIFE - DEER, OWLS, MICE, FOXES, BADGERS AND EVEN PERHAPS THE ODD GRUFFALO, CORNISH WOODLAND HAS A PLETHORA OF FLORA AND FAUNA TO TEMPT YOU AWAY FROM THE BEACH, OFF THE BEATEN TRACK AND ONTO A WOODLAND WALK.

Cardinham Woods near Bodmin is looked after by the Forestry Commission and hosts four trails (though there are miles of fun to be had should you venture off-piste, too). Woods Café, on the edge of the woods, is the perfect place to start - choose your challenge and reward yourself with some of their homemade goodies on your return.

From easy riverside walking, to climbing high-sided valleys filled with pine forest, the trails in the woods are suitable for walkers, dogs, horses, cyclists and explorers alike. Children love the freedom of a place like this.

EARN YOUR GRUB

LADYVALE VALLEY WALK
Super easy walk, picturesque and suitable for those with pushchairs. Earn a hot chocolate.

CALLYWITH WOOD WALK
Deemed a moderately challenging walk – a few small slopes. Earn a slice of home-made cake and pot of tea.

LIDCUTT VALLEY WALK
Also moderately challenging. A lovely long loop, perfect for a loping run or a march with friends. Earn a hearty sandwich and coffee.

WHEAL GLYN WALK
Hard. Plenty of slopes but the scenery more than makes up for the effort. Spot the old silver mine and engine house. Earn whatever you fancy!

CARROT CAKE WITH CORNISH CRÈME FRAÎCHE TOPPING

Its delicious squidgy nuttiness makes this easily the most popular cake at Woods Café. Lara Spurrell shares her recipe.

- 285g Cornish butter
- 285g light brown sugar
- 5 large free range eggs
- 225g self raising flour
- 285g grated carrots
- 1tsp baking powder
- 1tsp cinnamon
- 1tsp nutmeg
- ½ tsp mixed spice
- 115g ground almonds
- 115g chopped walnuts
- 70g sultanas
- Juice and zest of an orange

TOPPING:
- 60g very soft Cornish butter
- 50g icing sugar
- 300g Cornish crème fraîche
- Extra walnuts and orange zest to decorate

1 Preheat the oven to 180°C, grease and line a 9 inch cake tin.
2 Sift the flour into a large bowl, add the spices, baking powder and ground almonds. Stir until combined.
3 Using a hand held or free standing mixer beat the butter and sugar together until pale and fluffy.
4 Beat in one egg at a time, ensuring the mix is not curdling before adding the next. Don't rush this stage, it might take 10 minutes or so.
5 Add this to the flour and stir in gently until almost combined. Add the carrots, walnuts, sultanas, orange juice and zest and stir together.
6 Spoon the mix into the cake tin and bake for 1½ hours, checking after an hour with a sharp knife or cocktail stick. If the top starts to catch, cover lightly with foil.
7 While the cake is cooking make the topping. In a bowl beat together the butter and icing sugar until very smooth, then gently fold in the crème fraîche until just combined. Place this in the fridge for a least an hour while the cake cools.
8 When the cake is completely cold, spoon the topping onto the middle of the cake and gently push it towards the edges with the back of a spoon. Decorate with chopped walnuts and some orange zest.
9 Keep in an air tight box in the fridge for up to 5 days.

BLUSTERY DAYS AND WINTER WALKS

One of the best ways to embrace the Cornish winter is to take a windswept walk, ending up at a country pub, perhaps with a roaring fire, but definitely with a hearty warming lunch and a fine pint. Let the elements assault you as you navigate the miles of coastal path and country lanes, hopping over granite stiles and following grassy paths trodden, in some places, since the Bronze Age. With cheeks rosy and appetites growling, lunch will never have tasted so good.

An OS map is essential if you don't know your way, and wear plenty of layers, with a windproof one on top. The wild west of Cornwall is the perfect place to start.

WALK FROM PERRANUTHNOE TO PRUSSIA COVE

VISIT CORNWALL

Perranuthnoe is a pretty beachside village often passed by en route to the more well known destinations of Porthleven and Penzance. However it is one of Cornwall's hidden gems and a great starting point for a delightful walk of about two miles along the South West Coast Path to Prussia Cove. Take the path to the east from the car park at Perranuthnoe and it will open up to amazing views back across to St Michael's Mount.

If there is one cove in Cornwall whose story can fire up the imagination it is Prussia Cove. This coastline was home to the famous 18th century ship-wrecker and smuggler John Carter also known as the 'King of Prussia' after a childhood game he played. Along with his

brothers, Harry and Charles, John ran a smuggling trade from these coves which made him one of the most infamous of all Cornish smugglers. As you walk along the cliffs, especially on a blustery day, you can imagine his childhood games and get a good feel for Cornwall past. The sheltered coves have plenty of hiding places while the tide is in, and small picturesque beaches as it recedes.

As you come around the headland the main house is a Victorian retreat built in 1885 for du Boulay, a former Archdeacon of Cornwall in his retirement. Further along small former coastguard cottages are revealed.

The cove itself shows remnants of a small fishing trade with a large old winch above the high water mark. On the beach there are pools and caves to explore and play pirates as children have done since John Carter's first adventures.

For the return journey you can either head back the way you came and warm up with a well-earned lunch by the fire at the Victoria Inn, or you can head north inland through the lush Cornish fields in the direction of the Falmouth Packet Inn and perhaps sample one of their renowned roast dinners. Walk it off on the final leg back to your starting point.

CLASSIC ROAST DINNER

COURTESY FALMOUTH PACKET INN

A roast dinner in a Cornish country pub is what winters were made for. At the Falmouth Packet Inn, Rosudgeon, near Penzance, Matthew Rowe does a fab roast to warm the cockles on a brisk winter day, so who better to ask for some top tips for the perfect roast dinner?

MATTHEW'S TIPS FOR THE PERFECT ROAST DINNER

Despite being part of Britain's heritage, Sunday roast is one of those things that many people find daunting. The secret is all in the timing but here are a few other tips for the best ever roast.

- Buy meat from your local butchers and ask for their recommendations. They know what's best each week.
- Always buy the largest joint you can afford or reasonably use. Small joints don't cook so well.
- For beef, try rubbing some horseradish into the joint with the seasoning.
- Par boil potatoes before roasting and baste with beef dripping or a mix of cold pressed rapeseed oil and butter.
- For sweet honey-roasted parsnips, blanch before roasting with the potatoes. Drizzle with Cornish clear honey and glaze in a hot oven.
- For the best cauliflower cheese, blanch a Cornish cauli and dry on a clean dry cloth. Make a silky cheese sauce using three parts Cornish mature cheddar one part Cornish smoked cheddar and one part Helford Blue. Keep a little for sprinkling over the top before baking until golden brown.
- The secret of Yorkshire puddings... Cornish free range eggs are a must along with ice cold Cornish full cream milk and plain flour. Keep your batter very cold; oil your tins with fat drained off the beef, then preheat until they are smoking hot before pouring in the mixture (very carefully). Always bake in a very hot oven.

BEWITCHED IN BOSCASTLE

A COASTAL WALK ALONG THE SOUTH WEST COAST PATH THAT TAKES YOU TO BOSCASTLE, A NORTH CORNISH FISHING VILLAGE WHICH HIDES A WEALTH OF ROMANTIC HISTORY, SCENERY AND WITCHES!

The scenery around Boscastle is stunning, and the cliff path east of Boscastle towards Crackington Haven is a breathtaking roller-coaster hike, diving headily from high cliff tops down to deep green valleys. In the spring and early summer wildflowers are abundant: thrift, foxglove and campion will enliven your walk.

On your walk call in at the Boscastle Farm Shop and Café for a delicious homemade cake or a light lunch. The café is a short stroll from the coastal path with spectacular views of rolling hills towards the sea. Also stock up on local produce at the farm shop for a hearty post walk supper.

Not far from Boscastle Farm Shop a waterfall plunges down a craggy cliff at the head of the fjord-like Pentargon Cove. Seals frequent the rocks below and falcons nest in the cliffs above. The walk back to the café from the waterfall is challenging; a steep climb of a couple of hundred steps. Unless you are super-fit you don't have much choice but to take it slow and admire the delicate but plentiful heath spotted orchids if they are in season.

CORNISH EGG & BACON PIE

This traditional Cornish lunch or suppertime dish is good hot or cold and therefore also makes a tasty treat for picnics or lunch boxes. It's one of the most popular dishes on the menu at Boscastle Farm Shop. Jacky Haddy shares her recipe.

SERVES 6

PASTRY:
- 450g plain flour
- 225g Cornish butter cut into small cubes
- Pinch of salt
- Cold water to mix

FILLING:
- 450g chopped Cornish dried cured bacon – bacon scraps are fine
- 10 free range eggs
- Black pepper
- Chopped parsley
- Egg wash for glazing

1 In a large bowl, rub butter into flour and salt until it resembles breadcrumbs.
2 Add cold water to bind it and gently form it into a ball.
3 Chill in the fridge for ½ an hour.
4 Heat the oven to 180°C.
5 Roll out ⅔ of the pastry to ½ cm thickness and line a 26cm deep flan tin or pie plate.
6 Scatter the bacon on the pastry case.
7 Crack the eggs and space them whole around the outside edge of your case. If you have any left add 1 or 2 in the middle, sprinkle with pepper and parsley.
8 Brush around the pastry edge with a little beaten egg.
9 Roll out the remaining pastry and lift it over your pie to form a lid. Cut the edge to fit.
10 Press the edges firmly together and seal with your finger or a fork.
11 Glaze the top of the pie with beaten egg to give it a golden glaze.
12 Bake the pie in preheated oven for 40-45 minutes.
13 Leave to stand for 15 minutes before serving.

SUMMERTIME AND THE LIVING IS EASY...

HOT SUMMER DAYS, GOLDEN SANDS, TURQUOISE SEAS.
SUMMER IN CORNWALL SCREAMS BEACH BARBECUE.

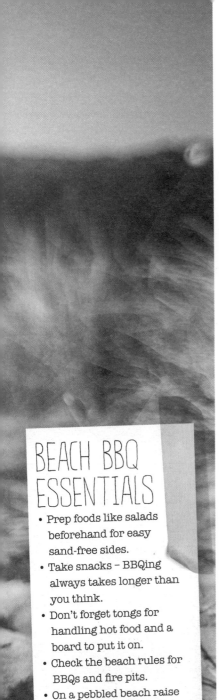

- Prep foods like salads beforehand for easy sand-free sides.
- Take snacks – BBQing always takes longer than you think.
- Don't forget tongs for handling hot food and a board to put it on.
- Check the beach rules for BBQs and fire pits.
- On a pebbled beach raise the BBQ off the pebbles, otherwise they will get hot and shatter.
- Douse any hot sand with cold water before you leave.
- Remember a bin bag and ALWAYS take all your litter home.

Once a strange habit practised by our antipodean and transatlantic cousins, this most egalitarian way of eating is now a firm favourite all over Britain - out come the barbies whenever the sun tries to shine and sometimes even when it doesn't.

A Cornish beach on a warm summer evening has got to be one of the best BBQ backdrops in the world. Soak up the dying rays, build up an appetite in the water, and unwind with friends and family as a tasty supper sizzles over the hot coals.

The only challenge is deciding what to cook. Spoilt for choice, it's the perfect opportunity for a mighty meat feast - succulent well hung steak, perky pork sausages (a robust flavour like garlic and red wine will come into its own), perhaps a juicy tenderloin of venison, or how about a bunny burger (lean, healthy and cheap – kids love them)?

For purists though, ocean-side grilling means only one thing - freshly caught fish. Not all fish stand up to this treatment, but for bright shiny mackerel it's perfect. Gutted and cooked whole, the oiliness of the skin keeps the fish moist and the smoke imparts that unmistakable open-air flavour. This is beach barbecuing simplicity at its best.

FARMING

IN ALL OUR FIELDS,
GOD SPEED THE PLOUGH,
THE PLOUGHMAN GUIDE AND KEEP
PREPARING BY HIS LABOURS NOW
AT HARVEST TIME TO REAP.

WORDS: TONY INGLEBY 2001

Farming shapes the land and the land shapes farming. Nowhere is that more apparent than in Cornwall, where the rolling hillsides that dominate the landscape create some of Britain's best terrain for grazing and growing.

This undulating, often steeply sloping landscape is characterised by small fields bounded by stone hedges and accessed via the narrow, winding lanes built by farmers of the past. Cornish farming was therefore never going to be able to adopt to any great extent the intensive post-war mono-culture systems that were designed for vast swathes of land and intended to ensure a plentiful supply of cheap food. What must have seemed like a disadvantage to Cornish farmers at that time, has happily come full circle and is potentially now their greatest strength. Cornwall's carefully balanced approach, working with nature rather than trying to outwit it, has stood the test of time and is now looking far more sustainable than the high-input systems that were once thought of as the saviours of the world.

Small fields with stone hedgerows are more than just quaint and pretty. Built from the large stones and boulders that were removed from the fields when they were first cultivated, Cornish hedges are the time-honoured and tested way of countering the prevailing westerly winds straight off the Atlantic. Animals that steadily graze the grassy slopes not only maintain the fertility and condition of hillsides sometimes inaccessible to machinery, they also produce much more flavoursome milk and meat than creatures subject to a more confined existence.

Cornwall's lower slopes are more sheltered and often benefit from the warm sunshine and frequent gentle rainfall of the county's numerous micro-climates. This is where you'll find veg in abundance – the Cornish staples such as potatoes, cauli and greens as well as more recent introductions like asparagus, courgettes and salads. Here and there, polytunnels hide the rich treasures that lurk inside – valuable crops such as sweet heritage tomatoes, micro-leaves and herbs, grown mostly for the restaurant trade; chefs and growers working in unison. This is where you'll find free range hens too, enjoying the good life of the Cornish landscape to produce golden eggs full of flavour.

At a time when provenance, traceability and quality are valued once again, Cornwall's farming has come of age.

EAT YOUR GREENS AND PURPLES AND ORANGES...

Mark Twain may have called cauliflowers "cabbage with a college education", but there's more to Cornwall's favourite brassica than that. They might not be the stars of the supermarket catwalk yet, but caulis are a staple of both the Cornish table and economy, for very good reasons. Bursting at the stems with flavour and nutrients, they store well and suit the mild climate perfectly – so when the rest of the country might be frozen under a blanket of snow, Cornwall can be relied upon to provide the cauli for the cheese.

It was the opening of the direct railway line from Penzance to London back in 1860 that meant fresh Cornish veg could be whisked to the dining tables of London for the first time. Riviera Produce, based near Hayle, started growing vegetables in Cornwall at about the same time and, although rail freight is now all but a thing of the past in these parts, they're still going strong. Working with 15 growers on family farms in West Cornwall, they're the people making sure that the county's cauliflowers and greens are on the shelves of Britain's supermarkets, fresh every day.

CAULIFLOWER SECRETS

- Cauliflowers can experience sunburn and may have a slight brown tinge if they are in the sun for too long. Much like our surfers!
- The 'head' is also known as the 'curd'.
- Cauliflowers curds come in more than just the snow white variety: they can be green, orange or purple.
- Cauliflowers were traditionally measured according to the size of a man's open arched hand, loosely placed on top of the curd.
- The leaves protect the curd. In winter, they keep the wind and rain off; in the summer they shade the curds to keep them white.

CREAM OF CAULIFLOWER SOUP WITH PRIMROSE HERD BLACK PUDDING AND TRUFFLE OIL

Tasty as it might be, there's so much more you can do with a Cornish cauli than cover it with cheese. Award-winning chef Stewart Eddy and his wife Anna run the Victoria Inn at Perranuthnoe, on the edge of cauli-growing countryside. This is one of Stewart's recipes for taking your culinary cauli know-how up a notch.

SERVES 6

- 2 Cornish cauliflower heads
- Some of the green cauliflower leaves, chopped
- Cornish butter and rapeseed oil
- 1 onion
- 2 sprigs thyme
- Vegetable or chicken stock
- Primrose herd black pudding, sliced
- Truffle oil
- Double Cornish cream and milk
- Salt and cayenne pepper

1 Roughly chop the onion and cauliflower heads. Sweat them in a little oil and butter with a pinch of salt and cayenne pepper without colouring them.
2 Add the stock and thyme to cover the veg, gently simmer until soft.
3 Liquidise the soup until smooth and pass through a sieve into a clean pan. Finish with a little double cream and milk, correcting the seasoning to taste.
4 Blanch the cauliflower greens in boiling, salted water and fry the black pudding in butter. Keep warm.
5 Pour the hot soup into a warm bowl.
6 In the centre, first place the greens, then the black pudding.
7 Drizzle with a little truffle oil and serve.

KNOW YOUR CORNISH VEG

SPRING GREENS

BEST EATEN – EARLY SPRING. **BEST COOKED** – STEAMED OR STIR-FRIED. **TOP TIP** – DON'T THROW AWAY THE STEMS, THEY CAN BE SWEETER THAN THE LEAF – JUST CHOP MORE FINELY.

CAULIFLOWER

BEST EATEN – WINTER AND SUMMER VARIETIES MEAN IT CAN BE EATEN ALL YEAR ROUND. **BEST COOKED** – IN THE OVEN OR POT-ROASTED. **TOP TIP** – THE LEAVES HAVE ALL THE FLAVOUR – DON'T WASTE THEM!

BROCCOLI

BEST EATEN – JUNE TO NOVEMBER. **BEST COOKED** – WITH STRONG FLAVOURS SUCH AS ANCHOVIES OR SOY SAUCE. **TOP TIP** – KEEP BROCCOLI IN THE FRIDGE TO ENSURE IT IS EATEN AT ITS BEST.

WHAT'S IN A VEG BOX?

THE BEDROCK OF THE ORIGINAL ORGANIC FOOD MOVEMENT, THE HUMBLE VEG BOX HAS REINVENTED ITSELF AND IS APPEALING TO A WHOLE NEW RANGE OF PEOPLE AND MOVING BEYOND ORGANIC. NEW-STYLE BOX SCHEMES INCLUDE FISH, MEAT, DAIRY PRODUCE AND EGGS, ALONGSIDE THE USUAL SEASONAL VEG OF COURSE, AND HAVE GOT TO GRIPS WITH THE DIGITAL AGE, WITH ONLINE ORDERING, RECIPES AND EVEN APPS TO HELP WITH MEAL PLANNING.

WHAT ARE THE ADVANTAGES OF A BOX?

- Getting fresher food that comes direct from the grower.
- Cutting down on travel costs with fewer trips to the shops.
- Letting someone else do the week's food and recipe planning for you.
- Saving money – you won't be tempted to buy food you don't need.
- Putting more money back into the local economy.

The Cornish Food Box Company started in 2010, vowing to sell only food that is grown, reared or caught in Cornwall. A tall order for the two sisters Tor and Lucy who run the business. So how do they do this 52 weeks of the year? Answer: by working with about 85 local producers – from farmers to bakers to fishermen – and by working hand-in-hand with the seasons. Each week's delivery is different and customers understand that there is more variety sometimes than others. It's nature and they live with it.

dig the EARTH & TEND TO THE SOIL

CORNISH NEW POTATOES

Cornish earlies are one of the first new potatoes to hit the shops. Potatoes have been grown in Cornish cottage gardens since the mid 1700s, when the potato and the pilchard were the staple diet of many Cornish families.

Best eaten – late April and May.

Best cooked – as simply as possible, added to salad or on the side with a bit of butter and black pepper.

Top tip – buy 'dirty' i.e. with some soil still on them – this preserves the quality, flavour and freshness.

ASPARAGUS

Eagerly anticipated, the coming of the asparagus season is one of the sure signs that summer is on the way. These succulent stems start to appear as the weather warms in late April, although here in Cornwall they've been known to arrive as early as March. Our benevolent climate and sea air is just what these warmth-loving, salt-tolerant plants adore.

Asparagus is picked for a strictly limited period of six to eight weeks. Extending the season is counter-productive as it simply deprives the crowns of their sustenance and produces a lower yield the following year.

GROW YOUR OWN

Imagine having your own plentiful supply of these precious treats. Cut straight from the earth, the flavour is unbeatable. It's not as tricky as you might think and, provided you follow a few ground rules, each crown can last up to 20 years.

- Be patient and don't be greedy. Buying year-old crowns will speed the process up, but you still need to wait until Year Two before cutting any spears.
- In Year Two, harvest the spears for just two weeks.
- From Year Three you can harvest for the full six to eight weeks. Aim to pick 250g – about the same as the bunches sold in the shops – from each crown each year.
- Keep the crowns well weeded and feed with a nutrient-rich mulch over the winter.
- Watch out for late frosts – they can be fatal if the spears have already started to appear. Gardeners' fleece will help to keep them safe on chilly nights.
- Asparagus loves good drainage. Add some sand, or even some bashed up bricks, to the bottom of the planting bed if necessary.
- To harvest, cut the stems with a knife, just below the soil surface. Never tug at them.

SIMON BURT

CHARGRILLED CORNISH ASPARAGUS, CORNISH DUCK EGG & CHORIZO

This recipe from Joe Lado Devesa, executive head chef at the Penventon Park Hotel in Redruth, is perfect for making the most of the short asparagus season.

SERVES 4

- 1 bundle/20 spears of asparagus, snap off woody end
- 4 Cornish free range duck eggs
- ½ tbsp extra virgin olive oil
- 120g chorizo, sliced
- White wine vinegar
- Cornish sea salt

1 Heat a pan with a little of the oil. When hot add the sliced chorizo. Sauté until they start to release their juices.
2 Bring two pans of water to the boil – one with a dash of white wine vinegar and the other with a good pinch of salt.
3 Place the asparagus into the pan of boiling salted water and boil for 2-3 minutes until cooked, but still with a bite.
4 In the pan of water and vinegar, soft poach the eggs.
5 To serve, place the drained asparagus onto the plate, place the cooked chorizo on top, then the poached egg. Drizzle with a little olive oil and serve.

TOP TIPS

- Asparagus contains few calories and little salt but is packed with vitamins and fibre.
- It is said to have aphrodisiac properties – maybe this is what made it wildly popular with the rampant Romans.
- Try dipping the spears into a soft boiled egg – sophisticated soldiers.
- Instead of chopping off the woody end of the stems with a knife, simply bend each spear and let it snap.
- Overcooking will ruin asparagus – either steam, or boil in lightly salted water for no more than three minutes.

PHILIP WARREN
THE MASTER BUTCHER

Perhaps because of his location, surrounded on either side by Bodmin Moor and Dartmoor, Philip Warren is one of the few butchers who recognise the quality and value of moorland livestock.

Livestock farming on the moors is in a perilous position because moorland animals, which can't compete with the large commercial beasts that have been bred specifically to produce more meat, tend to fetch a poor price. However, Warren's Butchers prefer the suckled native breeds from the moors. They're fed by the mother for eight months, then reared slowly on moorland heather and gorse and a healthy outdoors existence, yielding meat that is a glorious ruby red laced with fat the colour of Cornish clotted cream.

It's the quality of this meat that, coupled with the expertise of Master Butcher Philip, has been getting him a reputation others can only dream of. Warren's supplies around 20 Michelin starred restaurants including top London names such as the Ledbury and the Pollen Street Social, as well as the crème de la crème of the food scene in Cornwall, including the world renowned restaurants of Rick and Jill Stein and Michelin chefs Chris Eden and Paul Ainsworth.

Philip should know a thing or two about meat – his family have been graziers and butchers since 1880, with a shop in Launceston all that time. Could this be the oldest farm shop in England? Perhaps this is why he understands that being in it for the long term means working with farmers who in turn work with the countryside.

SGHAYWOOD PHOTOGRAPHY

WARREN'S -FIVE FAB- FORGOTTEN FEASTS

THESE ARE WARREN'S FIVE BEST 'FORGOTTEN' BEEF CUTS. THEY ALL NEED A BIT MORE OLD FASHIONED (OR IS IT 'NEW AGE'?) THINKING ABOUT THEIR COOKING BUT ARE GUARANTEED TO SAVE YOU £s WHILST STILL GIVING YOU LOADS OF FLAVOUR. AND WHO DOESN'T LIKE THAT?

FEATHER BLADE
A cut off the shoulder blade. Either cut it thin and cook it fast or go for the real slow option, for heavenly gravy.

SHORT RIBS
A slow braiser on the bone, with wonderful texture and immense flavour.

BOX EATER
A rolled joint off the front shoulder, needs longer cooking than topside but not as long as brisket.

BRISKET
Ideal for a slow pot roast, or the essential cut for making your own salt beef (think New York deli-style sandwiches...).

SHIN
The classic stewing beef, full of flavour.

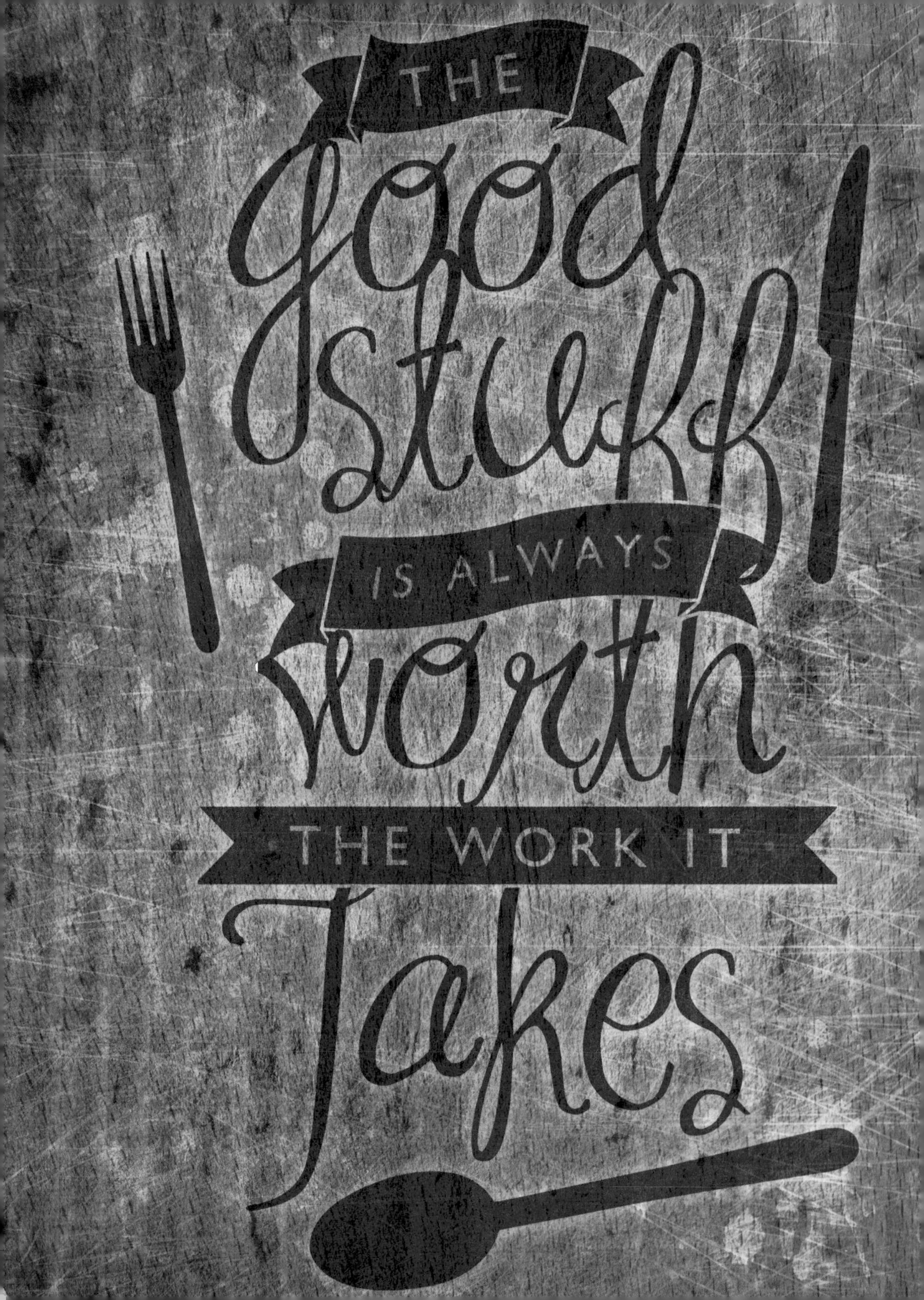

THE

good
stuff

IS ALWAYS

worth

THE WORK IT

Takes

PORK IS THE MOST VERSATILE OF MEATS, BUT MANY OF US DON'T VENTURE BEYOND SAUSAGES, BACON AND CHOPS. JOE SARDARI, HEAD CHEF AT BARCLAY HOUSE IN LOOE, HAS COME UP WITH THIS IMAGINATIVE WAY OF USING PORK TENDERLOIN - A LOVELY LEAN CUT. CIDER AND APPLES ARE CLASSIC ACCOMPANIMENTS TO PORK, GIVING THE MEAT A LITTLE SWEETNESS.

COURTESY BARCLAY HOUSE

CORNISH PORK BALLOTINE WITH BARBERRY AND HOG'S PUDDING STUFFING AND APPLES

SERVES 4

- 1 pork tenderloin
- 1 hog's pudding
- ¼ cup breadcrumbs, dried in the oven
- 2 tbsp barberries
- 1 egg yolk
- Cornish sea salt and pepper
- 2 red apples
- 2 tbsp sugar
- 1 tsp water
- 200ml Cornish cider

1 Soak the barberries in 100ml of the Cornish cider for 1 hour, then drain.

2 Trim the sinew from the tenderloin, then cover the meat with cling film. Bash it out using a rolling pin to about the thickness of a £1 coin. Remove the cling film.

3 Blend the hog's pudding, breadcrumbs, barberries, seasoning and egg yolk to make a stuffing, and spread it on top of the pork.

4 Roll the pork up around the stuffing into a sausage shape and tie using butchers' twine to create the ballotine. Poach for approximately 5 minutes in simmering water, then remove and leave to cool.

5 Peel, core and slice each apple into 6 chunky pieces.

6 Place the sugar and water into a frying pan and heat until you have a light caramel. Add the apples to the pan and cook for 2-3 minutes. Add the remaining cider and continue to cook for another 2-3 minutes - the apples should be cooked al dente. Drain off any excess liquid and cool to room temperature.

7 Untie the pork ballotine, season and pan fry until it is golden brown all over. Bake for 5 minutes at 180°C then leave to rest for 10 minutes.

8 To serve, cut into slices, about 2½cm thick, place the apples on top. Great with seasonal Cornish greens and creamy mashed potato.

GAVIN'S GUIDE TO LINKING SAUSAGES...

TOP TIPS

- If you are mincing the meat at home, put it through the mincer twice. It doesn't make it any finer, but helps mix the lean and fat together.
- Sausages need a certain amount of fat for succulence. Fat means flavour!
- Pork shoulder is about the right mix of lean and fat – 80/20 ratio – for sausages. Belly pork is good too, but will make a fattier sausage.
- Use your hands to mix the ingredients.
- Test a bit of your mixture for seasoning by cooking a little patty in a frying pan before starting to fill the sausages. Adjust and re-test as necessary.
- Don't overfill the skins – they will burst or be difficult to link.
- Always leave the made sausages to stand before cooking. This develops all the flavours properly and gives them the correct texture.

SAUSAGE-MAKING MADE EASY

DIY meat is on the up, and classes in how to butcher a carcass, prep your own piece of pancetta or reel off a personalised string of sausages have never been more popular.

Knowledge is power, as they say, and butchery knowledge is guaranteed to save you money and give you peace of mind about what you're eating, not to mention raising your kitchen cred to new heights.

How about trying the art of sausage-making in your own kitchen? There are very few hard and fast rules, so once you've mastered these basics from sausage pro Gavin Roberts of Kernow Sausage Co, it's guaranteed to become an infectious hobby as you experiment with different ideas.

The most important things you will need that you probably won't have lying around are a sausage-filling machine and sausage skins. A machine that's professional enough to give a good result, but small enough for household use, should cost less than £100. Why not share one with friends? You should be able to buy natural sausage skins from a friendly local butcher, or online.

TRADITIONAL WEST COUNTRY SAUSAGES

MAKES 4½KG

- 3kg boneless pork shoulder
- 1l chilled water
- 500g rusk or dried fresh breadcrumbs
- 4tsp salt
- 4tsp ground white pepper
- 20g ground coriander seed
- 10g dried thyme
- 10g finely chopped fresh parsley
- Optional: 3-4g dried garlic powder

1. Soak the sausage skins in chilled water overnight and rinse thoroughly both inside and out. Keep in water until needed.
2. Either mince the meat in a home mincer or ask your butcher to mince it for you.
3. Mix all the seasonings together, but not the rusk or breadcrumbs.
4. Mix the seasoning through the meat.
5. Add half the liquid and mix into the meat.
6. Add the rusk or breadcrumbs and the remaining liquid and ensure everything is evenly distributed.
7. Transfer the mixture to the sausage machine; place the sausage skins on the end of the machine and start filling.
8. For a professional finish, link your sausages – follow Gavin's step-by-step guide opposite.

LAMBING SEASON

Nancarrow Farm at Marazanvose has been in Pete Mewton's family since 1805. Pete decided to go organic 15 years ago and now Nancarrow is one of Cornwall's most well-known small family farms producing high quality meat to sell locally. The sheep graze on fertile land and in the winter they're treated to oats, turnips and hay grown on the farm, creating meat with the unique flavour that their regular customers love.

Pete has always got his eye on the sheep. Being brought up with farming he has an instinctive understanding of the animals and can spot problems early. This is an important part of organic farming where medical interventions such as the use of antibiotics are always the last resort rather than the first.

During the lambing season, days are long for Pete and his son-in-law Steve. The ewes give birth outside so a typical day starts with checking the fields for new lambs. The first couple of days is a critical time, so they are brought into shelter to make sure all is well and that they bond with their mother before going back out to the fields. One of the things Pete loves about farming is that life revolves around the seasons and every day is different. There are two lambing seasons at Nancarrow, November and February, ensuring fresh lamb is available all year round.

Pete's family has been at Nancarrow Farm for over 200 years and these days Steve and Pete are familiar faces at the farmers' markets in Truro and Falmouth every week selling the lamb alongside the farm's equally good organic beef.

Lamb in spring is mild, tender and juicy – the perfect match for salads and delicate spring veg such as asparagus and broad beans. In winter the meat matures to a darker colour and richer flavour, which lends itself beautifully to slow roasts and stews.

"Animals fed naturally on home grown food taste better and you get a wonderful diversity from it. It's the right thing to do."

HEAD CHEF TOM SCADE FROM TIDES RESTAURANT AT THE MARINERS IN ROCK WAS NAMED SOUTH WEST CHEF OF THE YEAR IN 2011 AND HAS A REAL TALENT FOR USING THE BEST CORNISH INGREDIENTS IN NEW WAYS. HERE HE CREATES A DISH USING CORNISH LAMB SHOULDER (FULL OF FLAVOUR AND GREAT VALUE) THAT WOULD BE IDEAL FOR AN AL FRESCO SUMMER SUNDAY LUNCH WITH FRIENDS.

BBQ'D SHOULDER OF CORNISH LAMB WITH RED ONIONS

SERVES 6

- 1 boned shoulder of Cornish lamb
- 1 head of garlic
- A handful of mint
- 10 peppercorns
- 150ml rapeseed oil
- 50g caster sugar
- 2 red onions, cut into eighths
- 25ml red wine vinegar
- 250ml red wine

1 Crush the garlic, mint and peppercorns in a pestle and mortar. Mix with the rapeseed oil, rub into the lamb and marinate overnight.
2 Take from the fridge an hour before cooking to bring up to room temperature.
3 Season and cook on a hot barbecue turning often. It should take 15 - 20 minutes to cook pink.
4 Wrap in foil and rest for 10 minutes then slice.

5 While the meat is resting, prepare the onion. Start by caramelising the sugar in a pan.
6 Add the red onion pieces and coat with the caramel.
7 Deglaze with the red wine vinegar and the red wine.

Try this dish with griddled courgettes and either Cornish early potatoes or, for a continental feel, make your own pissaladière. Roll out a rectangle of puff pastry and top with well caramelised onions, olives and tinned anchovies. Bake in a hot oven for 15 minutes.

Sunny Side Up

Eggs - what would we do without these small natural wonders? They're a perfect source of protein and one of the cheapest you can get.

There's miles of difference between an egg laid by a hen who spends her life indoors and one from a bird who gets to wander around the Cornish countryside. Just crack one next to the other and the difference will be startlingly apparent even before the taste test - the yolk of the indoor egg will literally pale into insignificance against the gorgeous dark orangey coloured free range one.

Fortunately, Cornwall is home to some of the best poultry farmers in England. The Tonks family of St Ewe Free Range Eggs is a prime example. Located on the beautiful Roseland peninsula, with its softly rolling hills, they bought their first 1,500 chickens in the 1980s after leaving dairy farming. Nearly 40 years on, numbers have grown nearly 10-fold and the farm's distinctive blue boxes can be spotted in shops, supermarkets and restaurants all over Cornwall and into the rest of the West Country. Michelin starred chef Chris Eden from the nearby Driftwood Restaurant even pops in to collect his own supplies.

Rebecca Tonks, who runs the farm with her parents, believes you only get good eggs from hens that live a good life. Nurtured on the farm from one day old, their hens join one of the small flocks when they're ready and are free to wander round spacious fox-proof runs with plenty of trees and shelter. Chickens are territorial, so each one has her own spot to perch each night. This means they are much more eager to roam outside in the daytime, safe in the knowledge that they have somewhere to return to sleep.

"Which comes first, the chicken or the egg? The chickens: we look after them and they take care of the eggs."

CORNISH GARDEN FRITTATA

PERFECT FOR SUMMER DAYS AND A GREAT VEGGIE TREAT

SERVES 3-4

- 125g small Cornish new potatoes
- 125g podded broad beans
- 100g soft Cornish goat's cheese
- 5 free range eggs
- 1 tbsp chopped fresh thyme
- 1 tbsp chopped fresh mint
- Cornish sea salt with black pepper
- 2 tbsp olive oil
- 125g chopped onions
- 225g sliced courgettes
- Sprinkle of thyme to serve

1 Boil the potatoes and broad beans (separately) until just tender. Shell the beans.

2 Whisk the eggs, cheese, herbs and seasoning.

3 In a large flat pan, heat the olive oil and cook the onions, courgettes, potatoes and beans, stirring for a couple of minutes.

4 Pour over the egg mixture. As the eggs cook push the mixture into the centre of the pan until set slightly, and then finish under the grill for 2 minutes, until golden brown.

DID YOU KNOW?

- Hens' eggs can come in a fantastic variety of colours from white and brown to blue, bluey green, reddish brown and speckled.
- Fresh eggs sink, older eggs float.
- In 1898 a book called "Eggs and how to use them" listed over 500 recipes.
- A hen takes 24-26 hours to produce an egg.
- Hens with white feathers and ear lobes produce white shelled eggs. Hens with red or brown feathers and red ear lobes produce brown shelled eggs.
- Hard boiled eggs spin, raw eggs wobble.
- Egg yolks are one of the few foods that naturally contain Vitamin D.
- One egg contains the same amount of protein as one ounce of lean meat, fish or poultry.

THE FULL CORNISH

TOP BREAKFAST TIPS

- Try flavouring the oil with sage. Heat the oil very gently and tear in 3-4 sage leaves. Leave on a very low heat for an hour. It's lovely.
- Slicing stem to base seems to be the fashion for tomato slicing at the moment, not through the middle.
- Make Fried Worms with bacon rinds. Cut off the rind with quite a lot of the fat left on it. Place in a small bowl; sprinkle with a little sage oil and a pinch of sea salt and bake in the oven until crispy.
- Do not prick the sausages.
- If you flip the egg over in the pan, you will end up with black bits from the bacon on it – not good.
- For a real Cornish twist serve breakfast with pressed Cornish apple juice.

HOG'S PUDDING

It's not a sausage, it's not a black pudding, it's not a haggis. It's sort of all three, but not any of them. Typically Cornish! Most butchers sell them already boiled, so they just need slicing and frying. Meaty, peppery, no two butchers ever make them the same. Recipes are closely guarded and handed down through generations, but when Sally and Bill Lugg set up the Primrose Herd of rare breed pigs more than 15 years ago, they were neither farmers nor butchers and had to learn from scratch. They must have found their true vocation because they've gone on to win probably more awards than any other Cornish pork farmer, including several for their hog's pud.

FORGET ABOUT LUNCH - BREAKFAST IS THE MOST IMPORTANT MEAL OF THE DAY. BREAKFAST IS ALSO THE BEST MEAL OF THE DAY - AFTER ALL, WHO HAS EVER HEARD OF AN 'ALL DAY LUNCH'? HERE ARE SOME ESSENTIAL TIPS FOR THE PERFECT CORNISH BREAKFAST, FROM HUGO WOOLLEY OF WOODLANDS COUNTRY HOUSE B&B, NEAR PADSTOW – A MAN WHO COULD COOK A GREAT BREAKFAST WITH HIS EYES CLOSED.

- At least 3-4 tbsp cold pressed rapeseed oil
- Half a large plum tomato
- Pinch of Cornish sea salt with chilli
- Few drops of Cornish Relish (like Worcestershire Sauce but sweeter)
- 1 slice of sourdough bread
- 1 tbsp of Cornish unsalted butter
- 1 traditional pork sausage
- 3 slices hog's pudding, skin removed
- 2 slices unsmoked back bacon with rind on
- 1 free range egg
- Freshly ground pepper

Set the oven at 190°C

1 Sprinkle some chilli sea salt and 4 or 5 drops of Cornish Relish over the cut side of the tomato and place at one end of the baking tray – to create 'Virgin Mary Tomatoes'.

2 Next, spread some unsalted butter on both sides of the slice of sourdough bread.

3 Cut the rind from the bacon - keep the rind.

4 Break an egg into a ramekin or a teacup.

5 Put a plate per person to warm. There is nothing more unpleasant than a hot breakfast on a cold plate.

6 In the preheated oven, put the tomatoes on the top shelf and bake for 5 minutes. At the same time put the frying pan on a low heat with a drizzle of oil. Fry the sausage gently for 2-3 minutes on one side and then turn for another 2-3 minutes.

7 After 5 minutes, check that the tomatoes are softening. Put the buttered bread slices on the same tray and put back onto middle/lower shelf of the oven.

8 Now put the bacon and hog's pudding slices into the frying pan with the sausage for 2 minutes each side.

9 Have some sheets of kitchen paper folded ready beside the hob. When the sausage, hog's pudding and bacon are nice and brown, pat the oil off on the kitchen paper, and put onto the hot plate to serve. Add a little more oil and pour the egg from the teacup into the oil. The oil should not be too hot; the egg white should slowly form without a rapid spluttering. The egg will gather some of the flavours of the bacon and the sausage. It is ready when the white has formed up to the yolk. If you want it 'over-easy' (as the Americans say) tip the pan and spoon hot oil over the yolk.

10 Take out the toasted sourdough croustade (ensure it is brown and slightly crispy), and the tomato. Place the tomato in the middle of the warm plate with the meat and place the sourdough croustade on the top of the plate. Lastly place the egg onto the croustade, a quick grind of black pepper on the egg yolk and serve.

HUGO WOOLLEY

THE RISE OF BAKER TOM

Young Tom Hazzledine's calling in life came more by accident than design. As a student he started working in a farm shop that was in need of bread. So Tom went home, baked four loaves and biked the bread back to the shop. It sold out. The next day he made more and that sold out too. And so he said goodbye to student life and began his new life as Baker Tom, a young entrepreneur leading Cornwall's rediscovery of real bread. Eight years on, he employs 30 people, has four shops and his wholesome and tasty bread and pastries are turning him into one of Cornwall's new treasures. With the baking bug firmly gripping the nation, Tom now also shares his self-taught skills with others in courses covering everything from how to make your first loaf to speciality baking.

LOVE LOAVES

BAKER TOM'S TIPS ON BAKING THE BEST LOAF AT HOME

- Use water that's on the cooler side in the mix. If it's too hot it will kill the yeast.
- Experiment with different flours, adding a little wholemeal or rye flour for texture and flavour.
- Take it slow – give the bread plenty of time to develop a fuller flavour.
- Make sure your oven is nice and hot (around 220°C).
- Place bread onto an upturned hot baking tray in the oven.

DID YOU KNOW?

- Cornish people traditionally ate a dark bread called maslin, made from barley.
- There are historically more than 25 different names for a standard tin loaf in Cornwall.
- Early bread ovens consisted of iron pots to cover the dough around which piles of hot ashes were placed.
- Later ovens were known as 'cloam' ovens and were made of clay. They were often heated with gorse.

"To make a small white loaf is about five hours from start to finish. It's all about the simplicity of the ingredients: flour, sea salt, fresh yeast and water."

CORNISH MILK

NOT ALL DAIRY IS CREATED EQUAL.
CORNISH MILK IS THE REAL DEAL.

It's easy to forget when you pick up a pint of milk that somewhere a farmer is making sure - come rain or shine, hell or high water - there will be more on the shelves tomorrow. However, even today, when it's tempting to think that producing food has become industrialised, great milk still begins with happy, healthy cows.

OUR COWS ARE OVER THE MOON

Cornish cows produce on average 1.5 million litres of the white stuff every single day, enough to fill 220 Olympic sized swimming pools in a year. This is the backbone of Cornish agriculture, responsible for about half of the county's entire farming output. But dairy farming around the globe has changed over the past 30 years and Cornwall is no exception. It takes half the number of farms to produce the same amount of milk as we used to and this has inevitably led to farmers moving out of the milking parlour and into new spheres. Throughout this book you'll see how this helped to stimulate Cornwall's food revolution, broadening the county's food horizons with new products and different types of farming.

But what of those family dairy farms that remain? For many, their survival has been assured by the success of other Cornish businesses that depend on their milk. One of these is Trewithen Dairy, set up 20 years ago by dairy farmer Bill Clarke and his wife Rachel. Convinced that people would prefer to buy milk that they knew had come from the cows they could see grazing around them rather than the anonymous milk that had become the norm, they set about bottling their milk on their own farm once their children were in bed. Sure enough it sold, as did the clotted cream they baked.

From those small beginnings, they have grown into Cornwall's third largest dairy processor, collecting up to 150,000 litres of milk every day, selling it to supermarkets as well as corner shops, cafés and restaurants, also turning it into a range of other delicious dairy products including, of course, classic Cornish clotted cream.

These days, their milk comes from 28 Cornish farms with an average herd of 150 cows, all located no more than 25 miles from the dairy. They work closely with each of their carefully selected farmers, making sure that the cows are well looked after and the milk quality is top notch. But Bill and Rachel haven't forgotten that dairy farming with all its unpredictability and the daily toil can be a harsh life. The success of their business is their way of helping to guarantee a sound and rewarding future for some of the dedicated farming families who deserve nothing less.

How to spot a happy healthy dairy cow.
Have a look in the Cornish fields for these five tell tale signs:
- *Bright glowing eyes*
- *A shiny smooth coat*
- *A moist nose*
- *Head held high*
- *Tail hanging straight down*

The cream of the crop!

Cornish clotted cream makes a day special

Clotted cream, along with the likes of the Cornish chough, engine houses, St Piran's flag, St Michael's Mount and long stretches of golden sand, is one of Cornwall's most iconic symbols and a dollop of Rodda's (a name surely familiar to almost anyone who knows Cornwall) is as lipsmackingly good today as it was over a hundred years ago.

Good old Cornish clotted cream has topped the scones of millions, including VIPs, royalty, and passengers on the last flight of Concorde. Today, it is sent to a large band of worshippers in places as far flung as Hong Kong, Japan and Dubai, to satisfy their clotted cream cravings.

So globally renowned is this Cornish delicacy, it has been granted special protection (PDO - Protected Designation of Origin) by the European Union, in recognition of the distinctive qualities that come from the rich milk of Cornish cows.

Rodda's may be a household name these days, but the company has grown from humble beginnings in the 1890s when Eliza Jane, great great grandmother of present MD Nicholas Rodda, made clotted cream and sold it to friends and neighbours, just like many other farmers' wives. She and her husband saw the potential in selling the cream more widely because visitors from outside Cornwall always seemed to adore it. As a result, Rodda's became the first Cornish clotted cream to appear in London, originally delivered in tins by train. This evolved into the innovative 'cream by post' concept, one of the first ever mail-order foods, enabling families all over the country to enjoy this Cornish treat wherever they liked.

DID YOU KNOW?

- Cornish clotted cream can only be made from Cornish milk.
- It was originally conceived by farmers as a way of preserving excess milk and was often used just like butter - for cooking and spreading on bread.
- It is believed that the recipe was traded with the Phoenicians when they came to Cornwall in 500BC seeking tin.
- The scalded milk left over from making clotted cream was excellent for fattening pigs and turkeys.

LIFE IS Sweet

NICE AND CREAMY

THE ECLECTIC WATERGATE BAY HOTEL COULDN'T FAIL TO
INSPIRE A CHEF TO CREATE GREAT FOOD. EXECUTIVE CHEF
NEIL HAYDOCK TRAVELLED THE GLOBE BEFORE LANDING
HIS LEADING ROLE AT THE HOTEL AND ITS SISTER CAFÉ
THE BEACH HUT, THAT OVERLOOK ONE OF THE MOST
BEAUTIFUL BEACHES IN THE WORLD.
   NEIL HAS SPENT YEARS DEVELOPING NEW IDEAS USING
HIS LOCAL INGREDIENTS AND HERE HE GIVES A CLASSIC
DISH A CORNISH TWIST BY USING LUSCIOUS CLOTTED
CREAM FOR EXTRA RICHNESS.

BEN ROWE

BEEF STROGANOFF

SERVES 4

- 150g shimeji mushrooms
- 500g trimmed Cornish beef fillet
- 1 medium onion
- 1 clove of garlic
- 1 bunch chives
- 50g gherkins
- 100g unsalted Cornish butter
- Cornish sea salt
- 100ml vegetable oil
- 2 teaspoons sweet paprika
- 50ml brandy (you could use white
  wine or Madeira as an alternative)
- 200ml Cornish clotted cream
- 1 lemon
- Tagliatelle or steamed rice

1 Prepare the shimeji mushrooms by cutting off the
stalk 2cm down from the cap.

2 Cut the beef fillet across the grain into 1cm thick
steaks, then cut into batons.

3 Peel and finely dice the onion.

4 Peel and finely crush the garlic.

5 Finely chop the chives and cut the gherkins into
batons.

6 Heat a large frying pan and add 30g of butter, when
sizzling add the mushrooms, lightly season with salt,
toss and keep them on a high heat for 30 seconds
before taking off and draining.

7 Wipe and re-heat the frying pan, add the oil. When
hot, add the beef in batches, turning until browned
on all sides but still rare in the centre.

8 Remove the meat into a bowl and wipe the pan
once again.

9 Heat the pan to a medium heat and add the
remaining butter followed by the onion and garlic.

10 Sweat this mix down until fully softened but without
any colour, this should take around 5 minutes.

11 Add the paprika and cook for a further minute
before turning up the heat and adding the brandy
which should flame.

12 Once the flames have gone out add the clotted
cream and a good squeeze of lemon juice.

13 Put the beef back into the sauce along with the
chives and check for seasoning.

14 Serve with tagliatelle or steamed rice with the
mushrooms and gherkins sprinkled over the top.

HOW IT'S MADE: CLOTTED CREAM

- Cream is first separated from full fat pasteurised Cornish milk.
- The clotting or 'clouting' happens when the cream is then gently baked for 60 – 90 minutes.
- A beautiful golden crust forms.
- The Cornish clotted cream is then chilled to develop its silky smooth texture.

Top tip: Add clotted cream to savoury dishes such as mashed potato, risotto and scrambled eggs for that added touch of luxury.

I SCREAM, YOU SCREAM, WE ALL SCREAM FOR ICE CREAM...

summer dream

The stuff of childhood memories, real Cornish ice cream is a heavenly treat, a reminder for many of halcyon sunny days adventuring on the beach or splashing in the surf. Its rich creamy dreaminess is mostly down to the lush Cornish milk and cream it's made from, and of course every Cornish ice cream maker will tell you they add their own touch of magic.

Take the Parkers, another Cornish dairy farming family, who learned the tricks of the ice cream trade almost 25 years ago, when they realised they had to adapt and diversify if they were to keep their dairy farm and provide enough of a living to bring up their children.

In a place like Cornwall, where the population can easily treble during summer, turning their milk into ice cream may seem like a no-brainer, but little did they know that their very own Callestick Farm Ice Cream would soon become a household name and a treat eagerly anticipated by holidaymakers year after year.

These days, they are still farming; still producing the milk that goes into their ice cream, ensuring that they control the quality right through the process. You can drop by the farm to see how it's made – and taste it for yourself, of course.

COURTESY CALLESTICK FARM

ICE CREAM MAKING TIPS

- Always use good quality ingredients, such as the best free range eggs you can get your hands on. This will turn your ice cream from good to exceptional!
- Cook the custard over a very low heat to stop the eggs over-cooking. If it gets too hot the mixture will curdle and turn into a very expensive scrambled egg.
- An ice cream machine is pretty essential. It's very hard to get a creamy smooth finish without one.
- Have your mixture very well chilled before you start to churn – it will speed up the freezing process.
- When making ice cream with colourful fruits like strawberries and blackcurrants, add a little lemon juice to retain a vibrant colour.

CORNISH CHOCOLATE MINT ICE CREAM

Discovering great ice cream is one of those 'Eureka!' moments, when suddenly you realise what you've been missing. If you're still searching, try making your own with this recipe from Tom Hunter, talented head chef at Cornwall's eco-hotel, the Scarlet, at Mawgan Porth. You won't be disappointed. The delicate flavour of the Tregothnan chocolate mint tea is just what this recipe calls for.

- 750ml whole milk
- 750ml Cornish double cream
- 450g caster sugar
- 20 free range egg yolks
- 15g Tregothnan chocolate mint tea
- Dark chocolate chips

1 Heat the milk, cream and tea until just simmering and leave to infuse overnight. Whisk the egg yolks and sugar together until the mixture starts to go light and fluffy.

2 Pass the milk mixture through a sieve to remove the tea leaves.

3 Warm the milk mixture and slowly pour over the eggs, stirring until it is all incorporated.

4 Pour back into a clean pan and cook on a low heat, stirring frequently. The mixture, known as a Crème Anglaise, or custard, is ready when it coats the back of a spoon.

5 Remove from the heat and place in an ice bath then chill in the fridge.

6 Churn, and store in the freezer – that's if you can resist eating it straight away.

Davidstow Crackler – A supreme cheddar with plenty of bite and exquisite texture. Extremely versatile, but delicious on its own; also makes the best toastie ever.

St Endellion – An indulgent, rich and creamy brie style cheese made using Cornish double cream. Ripens with a tang and a delicious squidge. Enjoy with a thinly sliced cured meat such as Deli Farm's wild venison bresaola.

Mature Cornish Gouda – Made by a Dutch farming family living in Cornwall , a cheese with a bit of a kick but still velvety smooth. Stands up to a robust chutney such as piccalilli.

Keltic Gold – A pungent, soft, creamy cheese washed in Cornish cider three times a week to give it a burnt orange, slightly sticky, edible rind. Eat with something as simple as a crisp juicy apple to enjoy the full flavour.

Allet – A mould-ripened goat's cheese aged for two weeks before wrapping. Mild, with a subtle characteristic earthiness. Good paired with summery veg such as asparagus and courgettes.

CORNISH CHEESE BOARD

SOFT AND SQUIDGY, HARD AND TASTY, MILD AND DELICATE. HOWEVER YOU LIKE YOUR CHEESE, THERE WILL BE A CORNISH ONE TO PLEASE. WE ASKED OUR FRIENDS AT NEWLYN CHEESE, A DELIGHTFUL CORNISH CHEESE AND CHARCUTERIE SPECIALIST, TO GIVE US THE LOWDOWN ON A SELECTION OF CORNWALL'S FINEST.

Cornish Blue – Intended to be eaten young, a soft blue cheese sometimes described as Cornwall's answer to Gorgonzola. The perfect partner for a Cornish vintage cider.

Cornish Yarg – Nettle-wrapped, delicate, fresh and creamy under its natural rind, slightly crumbly in the core. Great with fresh beetroot or a beetroot dip.

Bosvean – A Caerphilly style goat's cheese with a traditional dry and crumbly texture, subtle fruity taste and lovely nutty finish. Try with Kea plum jelly or quince cheese.

Helford Blue – A best-seller, made on the Lizard. Soft, creamy and full of flavour under a greyish blue knobbly rind. Delicious with a gooseberry compote or fresh figs ripened under the Cornish sun.

CORNISH YARG

Cheese is a staple part of our diet and the basic methods and equipment for making it have changed very little over time. However, over the last 15 years or so, something new has been stirring in the curds and whey: the rise and rise of artisan cheese, in which Cornwall, with around 40 different cheeses, has played a key part.

Cornish Yarg is probably the cheese people think of as distinctively Cornish and it was created in the 1980s in east Cornwall by Alan and Jenny Gray (Yarg is Gray spelt backwards). Now the home of this unique cheese covered in stinging nettles is in West Cornwall, where it is still carefully made by hand in open vats by dairy farmers Catherine and Ben Mead and their team of accomplished cheesemakers.

It's the mottled, lacy, green-blue hues of the nettle leaves, hand-picked and hand-painted onto the cheese, that fascinate people about Yarg. Rest assured, by the time this happens, the nettles have lost their sting via a gentle steaming process.

GRASP THE NETTLE

- Three tonnes of nettles are picked for Yarg every year, that's equivalent to two shipping containers.
- Prime nettle picking sites are a closely guarded secret.
- All nettles are picked and packed within 24 hours.
- A good nettle leaf is large and thick with no holes and no stem.
- An accomplished picker can harvest up to a kilo an hour.
- Nettles lose their sting once cooked or frozen.
- It's widely believed that they have antiseptic and anti-inflammatory properties.
- They are rich in minerals and vitamins A and C.

CAMILLA BIRD

Stinging nettle (Urtica dioica)

TRY THIS

The original Yarg's sister cheese covered with **WILD GARLIC LEAVES** instead of nettles imparts an oh-so-gentle but oh-so-moreish garlickiness. **PARTNER IT WITH PEARS.** Although grapes are often served with cheese they are usually far too acidic.

D No: 28

Name: .... Diana Nould......

cked: .... 11/05/20....

TR 208LL

yarg

yarg
CORNISH CHEESE
HAND-MADE NETTLE-COVERED CHEESE
EXCLUSIVELY PRODUCED BY LYNHER DAIRIES CHEESE CO. TRURO, CORNWALL TR2 4DX

THE MOOR – A PLACE OF MYTH AND LEGEND

The sweeping moorland of Bodmin Moor remains one of Cornwall's last untouched areas, with its prehistoric and medieval past there for all to see. Farmed for more than 4,000 years it's a dramatic landscape which has generated legends and folklore of ghosts and giants. Tales have passed down through the generations from King Arthur's Camelot to rumours of present day sightings of 'The Beast of Bodmin Moor'.

Although these days it may not be inhabited by smugglers and giants, the moor still evokes a feeling that time has stood still.

MOORISH CHEESE

THE VAST EXPANSE OF BODMIN MOOR LENDS ITSELF
TO THE PRODUCTION OF SOME VERY SPECIAL CHEESES.

CORNISH BLUE

Cornish Blue is made high up on the Moor, close to the ancient granite monument known, coincidentally, as the Cheesewring. In 2010 it beat over 2,500 other cheeses to be declared World Supreme Champion Cheese.

For dairy farmer Philip Stansfield, who knew absolutely nothing about cheese-making when he created Cornish Blue less than 10 years previously, it was the stuff of dreams and brought Cornish Blue instant recognition around the globe.

It was Cornwall's first commercially produced blue cheese, created intentionally to be different to other English blue cheeses. Softer, milder, a little sweeter, it nevertheless has that characteristic salty finish you expect from a blue cheese.

DAVIDSTOW CHEDDAR

While artisan cheeses have become increasingly popular, so too has good old Cheddar. But not as we know it. It's the extra mature and vintage Cheddars which leave a mouth-filling flavour that are leading the surge; so says Mark Pitts-Tucker, Chief Cheese Grader for Davidstow, Cornwall's largest dairy that sits on the northern fringes of the moor.

According to Mark, a good Cheddar has more complexity and intensity than just raw strength of flavour. A Davidstow Cheddar gives 'width and depth', delivering complexity and interest and leaves a creamy, long-lasting, pleasant aftertaste in the mouth and throat. Lesser cheeses tend to be 'narrow' and lack interest.

HOW THE BLUE GETS INTO CORNISH BLUE

- Starter cultures and liquid blue mould are added to milk which is constantly stirred. When the vat is full, rennet is added, forming a curd.
- After about an hour, the curd is cut into little cubes, along which the blue mould will form.
- The curd is stirred by hand, arms shoulder-deep, to remove the moisture.
- The curd is lifted out of the vat onto a cloth to drain. It is then placed into individual silver moulds and left to dry for four days during which time salt is rubbed into the rind.
- Cheeses then go to the maturing rooms for piercing which encourages the growth of mould along the cube lines and creates the signature Cornish Blue blue.

CHEERS!

SO, NOW I'LL SING TO 'EE
IT'S ABOUT A MAIDEN FAIR
I MET THE OTHER EVENING
IN THE CORNER OF THE SQUARE
SHE HAD A WILD AND ROVING EYES
WE MET DOWN TO LAMORNA
AND WE ROVED ALL NIGHT
IN THE PALE MOONLIGHT
AWAY DOWN TO LAMORNA

Twenty five years ago, you might have struggled to find a top notch Cornish beer. The cider was unspeakably rough in places, Cornish wine unheard of, and the mineral-rich water that springs here and there from the granite encrusted landscape was mainly used to quench the thirst of cattle.

All the more remarkable then that, from water to wine, Cornwall can now lay claim to one of the widest ranges of drinks anywhere, and the ideas just keep on coming. The latest, a premium Cornish gin from a brand new distillery, lifts the lid on yet another new dimension. It's a dynamic world, driven by fast-moving fashions and tastes and Cornwall is not only keeping step but pumping the pedal.

From the realms of Cornish drinks there are names that will be familiar to people all over the UK and beyond. Names like St Austell Brewery, 160 years old and steeped in history, but transformed to be at the forefront of modern brewing, alongside those like Sharp's, less than twenty years ago just a twinkle in someone's eye and now producing the UK's most popular draught ale.

Like the county's food, in every drinks category there will be some of the finest you'll ever have the pleasure of supping. To prove the point, scooping national and global championship awards has become almost a full time occupation for many and such is the demand that special lines and vintages regularly sell out. Cornwall's secret? A landscape and climate that lend themselves to the production of distinctive top quality raw ingredients, certainly, but more so, an atmosphere where the imagination can thrive. In every one of Cornwall's successful drinks businesses, from traditional mead made with Cornish honey to a new baby-pink soft drink made with rhubarb, there is someone with the skill, passion and inspiration to get the ideas flowing – and to put their finger on the winning formula.

CORNISH BOUQUET

Who'd have thought that this remote county in the far west of England would be as well known in some circles for its wine as it is in others for its clotted cream and pasties? Yet tucked in amongst the winding lanes and windblown hills are a number of award-winning vineyards creating white, rosé and red wines that make perfect bedfellows for Cornish food.

The trick has been the use of grape varieties that thrive in other parts of Northern Europe where the season is equally long and cool. They lend themselves to clean, crisp white wines and juicy, fairly light reds.

There's a steeliness to the whites, that the winemakers will tell you is something to do with the constant exposure of the vines to the salty coastal air and blustery winds. With subtle aromas and delicious acidity, they make a magnificent match for fish of all kinds.

The best-known Cornish wines are the ones that sparkle, and Camel Valley Cornwall Brut sets an impressive standard, outcompeting some of the best French fizz. Following in Camel Valley's footsteps, a number of other Cornish vineyards are paving the way to critical acclaim. Ones to watch are Polgoon Vineyard, on the westerly tip near Penzance, and Knightor Winery, a stone's throw from the Eden Project in the middle of the county. Both have attracted the attention of winemakers from the southern hemisphere, proving that Cornwall definitely cuts it on the international wine stage these days.

TRY THESE PERFECT PARTNERS

Knightor Winery's Pinot Gris – with a bowl of mussels in a rich cream or tomato sauce. Plenty of delicate fruitiness but enough acidity to balance the richness of the sauce.

Polgoon Vineyard's Sparkling Rosé – with crispy skinned roast chicken. With a lick of bubbles, the ripe berry hints have sufficient flavour and richness to pair a robust dish such as this.

Camel Valley Cornwall Brut – less is more with this sophisticated wine. It's an absolute treat paired with Fal oysters or sushi.

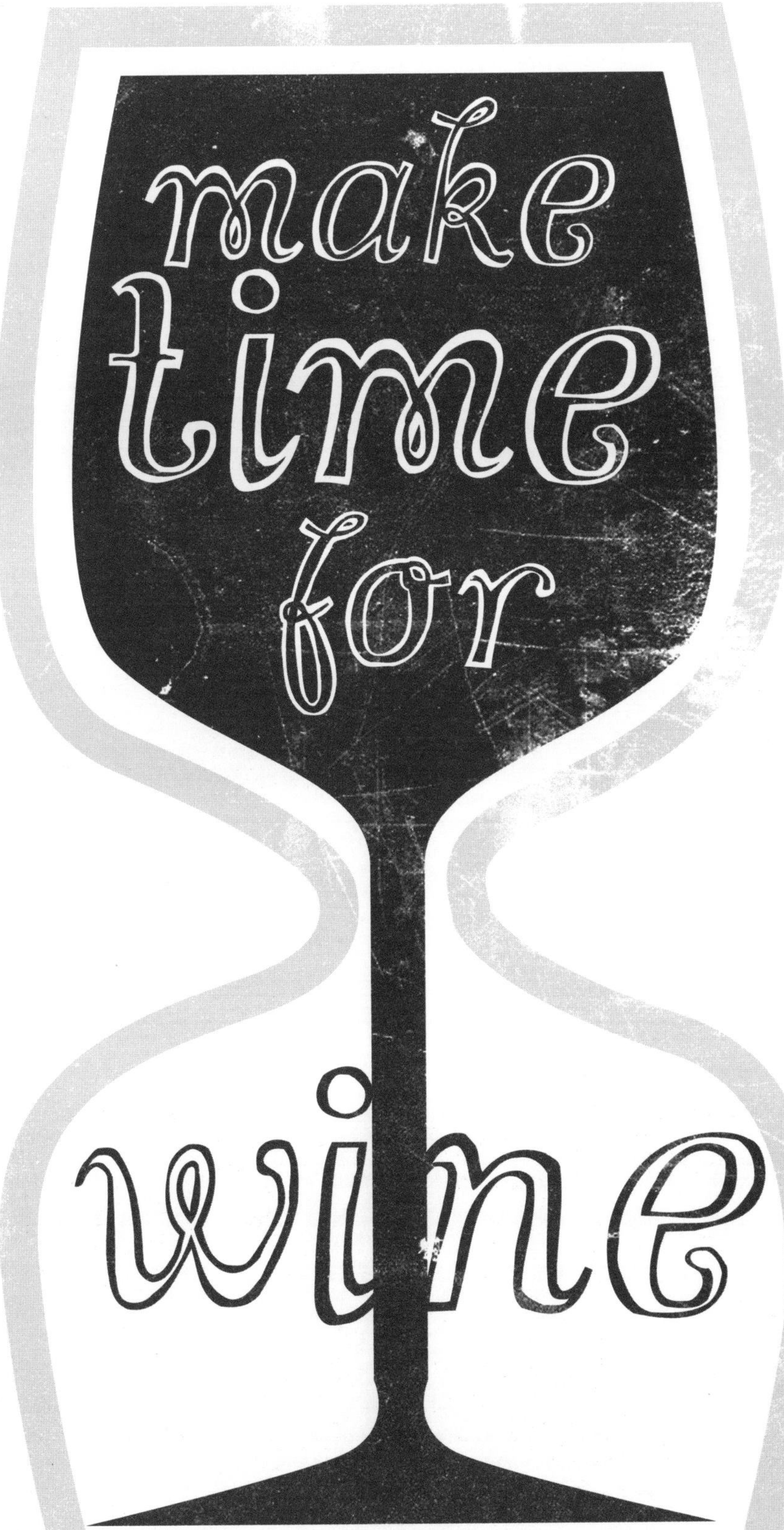
make
time
for
wine

THE MAN WHO FELL TO EARTH

HOW BOB LINDO'S PLANE CRASH LEAD TO
THE BIRTH OF THE CORNISH WINE INDUSTRY.

Bob Lindo is a man who understands challenges. A former RAF squadron commander who broke his spine ejecting from a plane in a mid-air crash, his enforced early retirement meant that he and his wife Annie moved to Cornwall with their family, with every intention of farming sheep and cattle.

He soon saw the potential of the sun-blessed, south-facing slopes in the sheltered Camel valley. Not only was the micro-climate good for healing broken bones, it offered ideal growing conditions for vines. And so began Cornwall's wine industry.

Over 20 years on, the 8,000 vines they started with has grown to 30,000, each hand-pruned and hand-picked throughout the year. A steady stream of people flock to the vineyard to see and hear how Bob, Annie and now wine-maker son Sam have beaten the odds and achieved world champion status. According to Bob, the challenges faced by UK winemakers are no different to anywhere else in the world: climate and soil.

"You'd be surprised how many customers say they first tried a glass of our wine at Tate Modern in London and felt they just had to come and visit the vineyard. I think making a top quality product is the secret of our success."

SO CAMEL VALLEY CORNWALL BRUT IS CORNISH CHAMPAGNE, RIGHT? WRONG! IN SO MANY WAYS:

- No sparkling wines made outside the Champagne region of France can be called champagne because the name is protected in EU law.
- Unlike champagne, every Camel Valley sparkling wine is a vintage. Reserve wines are not blended to produce non-vintage wines.
- Camel Valley Cornwall is best drunk young to appreciate the unique character of the grapes, with flavours reminiscent of elderflower and citrus. Champagne becomes rich and biscuity the longer it is aged.
- Champagne makers normally use Pinot Noir, Chardonnay and Pinot Meunier grapes whereas Camel Valley uses Pinot Noir, Seyval Blanc, Chardonnay and Reichensteiner.

A LITTLE BIT OF WINE KNOW-HOW

STORING AND TREATING WINE CORRECTLY IS OFTEN SEEN AS A BIT OF A MYSTERY. WE ASKED MICHELLE HUDD, SOMMELIER AT THE SCARLET HOTEL PERCHED ABOVE MAWGAN PORTH ON THE NORTH CORNISH COAST, TO OFFER A LITTLE INSIGHT.

SOMMELIER TIPS

- The best place to store wine is somewhere where the temperature is as stable as possible, preferably around 10-15°C – a garage or larder area is ideal. The kitchen, where most of us keep it, is probably the worst place to store wine.
- Try a chilled red. The Cornish reds are light enough to taste wonderful chilled. Perfect for a summer's afternoon on the beach.
- A white wine can mature faster and lose its fruit flavours quicker than a red.
- Don't throw away wine left in a bottle, or think that you have to finish the whole bottle once you've started it: it will last for 2-3 days.

A year in the life of a Cornish vineyard

JULY
fruit set

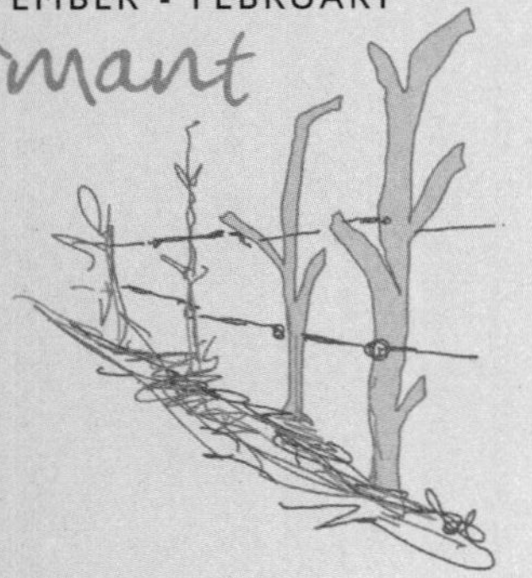

NOVEMBER - FEBRUARY
dormant

JUNE - JULY
flowering

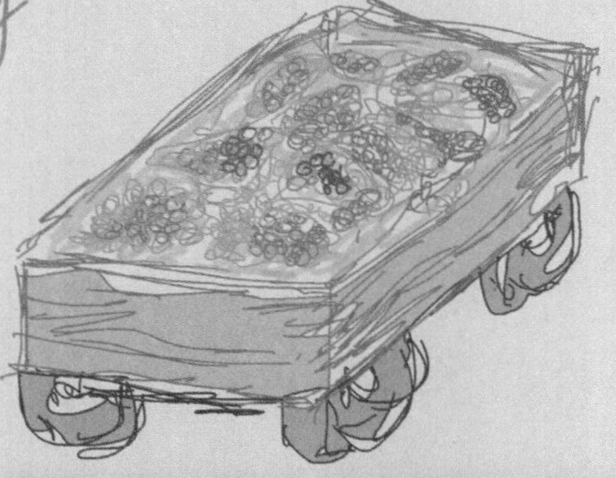

SEPTEMBER - OCTOBER
harvest

MARCH - APRIL
weeping bud burst

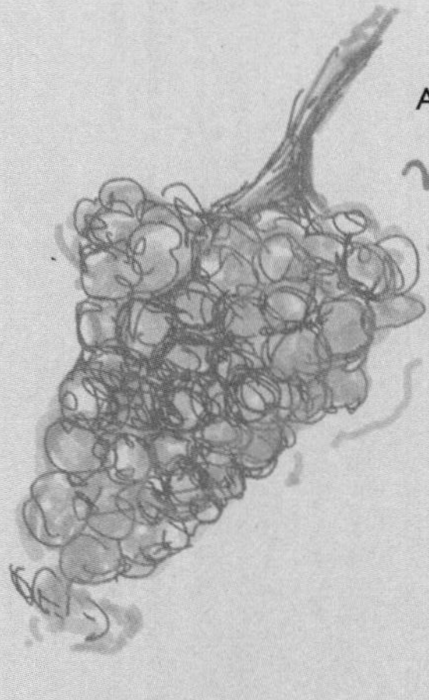

AUGUST - SEPTEMBER
ripening

THE HARVESTING PROCESS

The first apples are picked in late summer and harvesting continues through the autumn. At Cornish Orchards, apples are sent bobbing along an ingenious 'river' of water that replaces the need for a fork lift truck by carrying them direct into the pressing area, where they are washed and milled into a pomace – the ground up apple mixture. The press then squeezes out the juice which is either bottled straight away for a refreshing non-alcoholic drink or fermented for cider using wild and dried yeasts to maintain the flavour.

CIDER HOUSE RULES

THERE ARE FEW THINGS SO REFRESHING AFTER A GLORIOUS SUNNY DAY WALKING THE MOORS, EXPLORING THE WOODLAND OR SURFING THE ATLANTIC, AS AN ICE COLD GLASS OF CORNISH CIDER. A TRADITIONAL PALETTE TINGLER, CIDER IS A GREAT WESTCOUNTRY FAVOURITE AND IT'S GREAT TO COOK WITH TOO.

Someone who knows about the complexities of cider-making in the 21st century is Andy Atkinson of Cornish Orchards, near Looe in South East Cornwall. Previously a dairy farmer, he changed track in 2000 and soon discovered the knack for getting the quality and flavours of his cider and apple juice spot-on. It's as complex as wine-making – apples have variable tannins, sugar, astringency and depth of flavour, just like grapes. For Andy, it's all about the balance of sweetness and acidity and he still insists on checking every batch personally before giving it his seal of approval.

Cornish apple varieties have evolved to grow best in Cornwall's challenging conditions of fairly poor, steep ground and thin acidic soil. Cidermakers seek out these nuggets of sweetness that often have intense, concentrated and distinct flavours, using them to create unique and special blends.

CORNISH MUSSELS WITH CIDER BRANDY AND SHELLFISH BROTH

NICK HODGES, EXECUTIVE HEAD CHEF AT THE FLYING FISH RESTAURANT IN HIS HOME TOWN OF FALMOUTH, GIVES PLUMP CORNISH MUSSELS A BIT OF A TWIST. HEAVY ON FLAVOUR BUT LOW ON CALORIES. WHAT MORE COULD YOU ASK FOR?

SERVES 2

- ½ kilo of Cornish mussels - de bearded and cleaned
- 50g crayfish tails or prawns (lobster if you are feeling really generous!!)
- Chopped dill and parsley
- 250g roughly diced mix of carrot, onion, celery and fennel
- 2 fresh tomatoes, rough chopped
- 2 garlic bulbs, rough chopped
- 500g shellfish bones; lobster, prawns, langoustine etc
- Large shot of apple brandy
- ½ pint Cornish cider
- 25g Cornish butter

1 In a thick-bottomed saucepan cook the vegetables in the butter without colouring them.
2 Add the shellfish bones; continue cooking for approximately 10 minutes.
3 Turn up the heat and add the brandy. Allow the brandy to flame as this cooks off the alcohol and stops the finished sauce tasting bitter.
4 Add the cider and the stalks of the dill and parsley.
5 Add enough water to just cover the vegetables and bones. Cover and cook slowly for 10 minutes.
6 Remove the lid and reduce the stock by ½.
7 Strain the vegetables and bones leaving a clear and flavoursome shellfish broth.
8 Heat a pan large enough to take all the mussels.
9 Make sure the pan is very hot.
10 Add the cleaned mussels, they should start to open very quickly if your pan is hot.
11 Add the shellfish stock and cover for 3 minutes. Remove the lid, check that all the mussels are fully open, cook for a little longer if necessary.
12 When all the mussels are open (discard any that don't open at all) add the chopped herbs and the prawns or similar shellfish. Heat for 1 minute, check the seasoning, serve.

CIDER STYLES AND PAIRINGS

FARMHOUSE CIDER
The traditional way in which West Country cider was made; many would call this 'real' cider. Always still, never fizzy, the timeless accompaniment to a ploughman's lunch.

VINTAGE CIDER
Generally made from a single year's pressing of traditional cider apples, vintage cider is full bodied and strong. It needs a robust food such as mackerel to stand up to it.

SPARKLING CIDER
The most popular type of cider today. Served ice cold it's classically quaffable on warm summer days. Try it with cured meats such as coppa ham.

PEAR CIDER
Delicate but refreshing, modern pear cider is made from dessert pears rather than traditional perry pears producing a much gentler drink with a crisp finish. Ideal served in a wine glass to accompany seafood.

BLUSH CIDER
A bright and bubbly cider, perfect for celebrations. Serve in a flute as a fruity pink fizz. Goes well with chocolate or pavlova.

CORNISH BLUSH CIDER AND RASPBERRY JELLY

Nick Barclay runs Blue Plate at Downderry, close to Cornish Orchards. So when we asked him for a recipe using cider, he had no problem coming up with this ingenious dessert, perfect for a summer day.

COURTESY BLUE PLATE

SERVES 4
- 500ml Cornish blush cider
- 24 raspberries
- 30g caster sugar
- 4 leaves gelatine
- Cornish double cream
- Mint for decoration
- Cookie or biscotti for garnish

1 Pour the cider into a pan with the sugar and 12 raspberries, bring to a gentle boil and lightly simmer for 5 minutes until the raspberries are very, very soft.
2 Take off the heat and pass through a fine sieve.
3 Soak the gelatine in room temperature water until soft, squeeze out excess water and add to the blush/raspberry juice. Stir until the gelatine has completely dissolved in the juice.
4 Pour juice into chosen glasses and place in the fridge for an hour or two to set.
5 Pour a thin film of double cream on top and decorate with raspberries, mint and cookie.

CORNWALL'S REMOTENESS & ITS MANY **MICRO-CLIMATES** RESULTED IN VARIETIES OF **APPLE** THAT WERE **UNIQUE** TO THE COUNTY...

64

Cornish apple varieties have been recorded

Cider Isn't Just For A pint in the pub. Enjoy with a meal served in a wine glass

IT WAS USUAL FOR **FARM WORKERS** TO DRINK UP TO **3** OR **4** PINTS A DAY JUST FOR **REFRESHMENT**

MAKE MINE A PINT!

Beer comes third on the list of the world's most popular drinks after water and tea and was historically one of the most important components of a Cornishman's daily diet. The very process of brewing made beer one of the safest things to drink for hundreds of years, safer even than water. Moreover, it was a form of refreshment that quenched the palates of nobility and peasants, miners and farmers, lawyers and landowners alike.

The humble pint is now being lifted beyond the bar to the table. Beer tasting is now an art form; chefs are incorporating it into their cooking, restaurants are pairing it with food and, if current trends are anything to go by, beer lists will soon be as long as wine lists.

Cornwall is doing its bit in that revival and proudly boasts three heavyweights of the beer world: Sharp's, Skinner's and St Austell Brewery, whose excellent beers include celebrated favourites like Tribute and Doom Bar, enjoyed across and beyond the UK.

The name of a local pint is often rooted in Cornish identity. Landmarks such as the treacherous Doom Bar in the Camel Estuary, folkloric characters such as Betty Stogs, and heroes such as Trelawny all lend their names to popular brews, while Korev (St Austell Brewery's lager) is the word for beer in the Cornish language. Beery homage is also paid to a more recently famous Cornish character, Rick Stein's much-missed dog Chalky (look for Sharp's Chalky's Bite and Chalky's Bark), while Skindog lager celebrates the county's famous pastime and champion surfer, Ben Skinner.

Cornwall's brewing success is good news for farmers too. Brewers need barley and are working with local farmers to grow more to keep pace with the rapidly increasing popularity of Cornish beers. Keeping it local like this means that farmer and brewer can work hand-in-hand.

MIKE NEWMAN

DID YOU KNOW?
St Austell Brewery, established in 1851, is one of the oldest family-owned independent breweries in the UK.

WHO WAS BETTY STOGS?

According to Cornish folklore, Betty Stogs was unkempt and lazy and preferred a drop of ale to cooking, cleaning or mending. Her apparent reform came after the fairies visited and took her baby away one morning, only to return it clean and laid upon a bed of moss.

Today, a much more diligent Betty Stogs can be found collecting for charity at nearly all the community events that Skinner's Brewery supports.

WHAT MAKES CORNISH BEER SO GOOD?

A KEY AND FUNDAMENTAL INGREDIENT THAT HELPS DEFINE THE QUALITY OF A CORNISH PINT IS WATER.

- A lot of breweries source it straight from a spring.
- Most Cornish water is soft which is great for lighter European style beers.
- Soft water can be easily altered to become hard which is more suitable for stout.
- Spring water is high in minerals but varies greatly from place to place, helping each beer to develop its own unique flavour.

CORNISH STEAK AND 1913 STOUT PIE

ST AUSTELL BREWERY'S HEAD BREWER ROGER RYMAN RESURRECTED AN OLD 1913 STOUT RECIPE WHICH HE FOUND IN THE BREWERY'S ARCHIVED JOURNALS, FAITHFULLY KEPT BY THE ST·AUSTELL BREWERS OVER THE DECADES. AND, AS THEIR DEVELOPMENT CHEF NICK HEMMING FOUND OUT, THE STOUT WORKS EXTREMELY WELL IN THIS MOUTH-WATERING PIE, GIVING IT A FABULOUSLY RICH FLAVOUR.

SERVES 4

PASTRY:

- 300g plain flour, plus extra for rolling out
- 100g unsalted Cornish butter cubed
- 100g shredded suet
- Pinch of Cornish sea salt
- 125ml cold water

FILLING:

- 750g Cornish braising steak / shin or skirt, cut into chunks
- 150g chopped streaky bacon
- 600ml of St Austell`s 1913 stout or HSD (soak the beef in the stout overnight)
- 3 tbsp plain flour
- Salt and freshly ground black pepper
- 3 tbsp olive oil
- 2 garlic cloves crushed
- 200g whole baby onions
- 1 fresh or dried bay leaf
- Handful fresh thyme sprigs
- 1 tbsp tomato purée
- 1 tbsp balsamic vinegar
- 400g chestnut or white mushrooms cut into quarters
- Beaten egg to glaze

1 For the pastry, add the flour, suet, butter and a pinch of salt into a bowl and use your finger tips to rub the fat into the flour until it resembles breadcrumbs. Stir in the cold water, gently bringing it together. Alternatively blend all ingredients in a food processor and slowly add the water. Wrap the pastry in cling film and place in the fridge for later.

2 For the filling, drain the beef from the stout (keeping the liquid to one side) and pat dry with a clean towel, then mix the beef with the flour and some salt and pepper. The best way to do this without making too much mess is to put everything into a large food bag, seal, and shake.

3 Heat a tablespoon of the oil in a large pan up to a high heat, shake off the excess flour from the beef and, keeping the chunks well-spaced, fry until golden-brown all over.

4 Transfer the meat to a bowl, then add a splash of stout to the pan and scrape up any meaty bits. Tip the liquid into the bowl of meat. Wipe out the pan, then add a tablespoon of oil with the bacon, garlic, onions, mushrooms and herbs and fry to soften for a few minutes.

5 Put the beef back into the pan. Pour in the stout, then add the tomato purée and balsamic vinegar. If necessary, add a little hot water to ensure the meat is covered in liquid (this will prevent the beef from drying out). Bring to the boil, skimming off any impurities, then cover and simmer the stew for 1-1½ hours until the beef is almost tender and the sauce has thickened.

6 Set aside to cool, overnight if possible.

7 To make the pie, preheat the oven to 200°C. Flour the work surface, then roll out the pastry until it is roughly 1cm thick and a little larger than your pie dish.

8 Put the filling into a pie dish and brush the edges with a little water or beaten egg.

9 Place the pastry on top by laying the pastry over a rolling pin to lift it. Press down gently to seal.

10 Cut a couple of slits in the top of the pie to release steam. Brush the top of the pie with beaten egg.

11 Bake for 30 minutes, or until the filling is bubbling and the pastry is golden-brown all over.

CORNISH MICROBREWERIES

Craft beers are on the up everywhere it seems, as people seek out the creativity and authenticity of the small scale entrepreneurs, but nowhere are they more popular apparently than here in Cornwall. Word on the street is that there are more breweries per capita here than any other county in the UK.

There was a time when small scale brewing conjured up images of enthusiasts in dusty garages. Now it's entered a whole new realm, with slick operators producing traditional brews alongside new and lighter continental and American influenced beers that suit the sunshine and lifestyle of Cornwall and appeal to a much broader range of tastes.

BEER AND FOOD PAIRINGS FROM THE MICROBREWERS

You name the food and there is almost certainly a Cornish microbrew to partner it. Try these ideas:

Imperial Chocolate Stout, 8.7% ABV, Harbour Brewing Co: Cocoa nibs in the brew give this beer a richness that goes well with chocolate brownies or dark chocolate mousse, topped with Cornish clotted cream, of course.

Magik, 4% ABV, Keltek Brewery: A classic 'best' bitter, with the traditional flavours of malt and hops shining through. Makes an ideal partner for a classic dish of beer-battered fish and chips.

Monks Brew, 6.4% ABV, Penpont Brewery: An abbey style, dark beer, brewed with juniper for a distinctive flavour. Slightly sweet. A great match for slow-roasted Cornish moorland lamb.

Cornish Sunset, 4% ABV, Rebel Brewing Co: A crisp and refreshing golden ale. Citrus and fruity notes make this beer a perfect partner for a fresh Cornish crab sandwich or a seafood platter on a summer's day.

JAMES RAM

BEER BATTERED FISH & CHIPS

KIT DAVIS AT THE CASTLE RESTAURANT IN BUDE GIVES THIS CLASSIC DISH A TWIST USING REAL ALE IN THE BATTER TO ADD FLAVOUR AND A LOVELY LIGHTNESS.

MOWENNA PHOTOGRAPHY

- 500 ml Cornish Ale
- 100ml Cornish sparkling water
- 350g plain flour
- 4 portions Cornish pollack, skinned and boned
- 6 large washed Cornish potatoes
- Cornish sea salt to season

SAUCE GRIBICHE:
- 6 tbsp mayonnaise
- 2 tbsp chopped gherkins
- 2 tbsp chopped capers
- 2 tbsp chopped tarragon
- 2 tbsp chopped parsley
- 1 grated hard boiled egg
- ½ red onion – finely sliced
- ½ clove garlic – finely diced
- Squeeze of lemon

METHOD
1 Make the Sauce Gribiche simply by combining all the ingredients.
2 Whisk flour and ale together. Gradually add sparkling water until the mixture reaches the consistency of single cream.
3 Cut the potatoes into chunky chips. Deep fry the chips at 125°C until soft (around 5 minutes). Turn the fryer up to 180°C. You are now ready to cook your fish and chips.
4 Lightly flour the fish and dip in the batter until fully coated.
5 Gently place into the fryer (make sure the basket is down before placing fish into the fryer). Once the batter around the fish is sealed, drop in the chips. Cook until all is golden brown and the fish is hot in the middle - you can check this with a knife.
6 Drain excess oil on a plate lined with kitchen roll and season with Cornish sea salt.
7 Serve with a wedge of lemon and Sauce Gribiche.

LEARN THE LINGO

Ale – historically a beer brewed without hops, but now refers to beer made with malted barley. All ales are beers but not all beers are ales.

Craft ale – can refer either to ales made by microbreweries or to speciality ales made by larger breweries but in limited volumes.

Lager – refers to the production method (from the German word 'to store') of slow fermentation at low temperature. Lagers are usually served chilled and are the most popular style of beer in the world.

Microbrewery – small-scale, artisan, independent brewer.

THE CORNISH WAY

I DEARLY LOVE A PASTY, A 'OT LEAKY ONE:
WITH MAYT, TURMIT 'AND TATY H'ONYON
AND PARSLEY IN 'UN. THE CRUS' BE MADE
WETH SUET, SHAPED LIKE 'ALF A MOON:
CRINKLY H'EDGES, FRESHLY BAKED 'E ES
ALWAY GONE TOO SOON!

Wherever you go in the world, food is far more than nourishment and sustenance; it's part of the culture and the way of life.

Here on this slice of land at the end of Britain, a finger jutting out into the Atlantic, the culture (and the food) is alive and kicking and making waves. In common with other peripheral places, it's easy for a strong identity to thrive here, but Cornwall is a place where a proud sense of heritage goes hand-in-hand with entrepreneurial spirit. That's why Cornish pasties and clotted cream are still the county's most iconic foods, but have evolved to find their place in the 21st century and are now part of a Cornish food and drink picture that includes influences from all over the world. Home-grown tea, charcuterie, patisserie, granola, cold pressed oil, wine, lager. You name it, if it's doable, Cornwall has probably got it. It's an eclectic mix, reflecting the constant influence of inward and outward travel on the local style, which saves 'traditional' becoming a by-word for 'old fashioned'.

Throughout history, Cornwall has been a place that inspires creativity and Cornish people have become adept at exploring new ideas, often to survive. Nowadays chefs, retailers and even wholesalers and manufacturers sit down with farmers and growers and plan their calendars together, working out the art of the possible, giving things a go. They fill the gaps so that as much as possible of their shopping list is produced nearby. It's classic win-win.

The Cornish way of life is also characterised by its deep-rooted, down-to-earth, relaxed nature. This is why you'll find hotels, restaurants, cafés and pubs all over Cornwall that ooze style without a hint of ostentation. It's a perfect fit for today's informal lifestyles and is one of the main reasons why Cornwall is the height of contemporary coolness.

If the secret of success in the food and drink world is having the right people with the right ingredients in the right place at the right time, Cornwall's time has surely come.

OGGY!
OGGY!
OGGY!

TIN-MINERS' WIVES OR PASTY SELLERS SUPPOSEDLY SHOUTED "OGGY-OGGY-OGGY" –
THE RESPONSE FROM ANY HUNGRY MINER OR LABOURER WOULD BE OI!, OI!, OI!.

HISTORY OF THE PASTY

If there is one thing that binds the Cornish, and one thing that can separate them pretty quickly it is the pasty. A 'national dish', symbol of the South West, export and staple a good pasty has no equal. Ask a group of people from Cornwall who makes the best pasties in the land and you will incite a humourous yet passionate argument as the names of bakeries, friends and relatives are put forward and products eulogized and defended with comical vigour. A pasty is more than a fancy pie. With perfect pastry, secret ingredients and the freshest of skirt and veg, a 'proper' Cornish pasty is a work of art.

Pasties are thought to have been around in Cornwall since the 14th century so it's only natural then that the Cornish have become rather attached to them.

Originally a good, calorie-filled, transportable meal for hungry workers – possibly even the first real 'convenience' food - it would have contained cheap ingredients such as potato, swede and onion without the succulent meat that is included in pasties today. That came later as people became bigger meat eaters and pasties became more widely eaten.

It was the advent of Cornish mining in the 19th century that really brought the pasty into its own and made it an important part of the life of so many Cornish families. Pasties were taken down the mines by the adults and children who worked there; the shape and size made them ideal for carrying, and they became the staple for the daily crib or croust – Cornish dialect for a bite to eat, usually taken mid-morning. It is thought that the miners gave the pasty its distinctive D shape too – the crust became a handle, which was discarded to prevent contaminating the food with grubby, possibly arsenic-ridden hands. Others will dispute this, arguing that miners ate their pasties wrapped in muslin or paper bags so that they could enjoy every last bit, as we do today. Miners would also often leave a bit of the crust on rocky shelves in the mine to curry the favour of 'the knockers' – the little mischievous people who lived below the ground.

For many families, pasty-making was an almost daily task and recipes were handed down from mothers to daughters, rarely written down. Producing a fine pasty takes a certain knack and many cooks take pride in their pasties, so much so that not many pasty makers will share their actual recipes, and some have taken them to the grave refusing even to pass them onto their offspring.

DID YOU KNOW?

In 2006 select mining landscapes across Cornwall were inscribed as a UNESCO World Heritage Site, placing Cornish mining heritage on a par with international treasures like Machu Picchu, the Taj Mahal and the Great Wall of China.

CORNISH PASTY RECIPE

SERVES 4

FOR SHORTCRUST PASTRY

(rough puff can be used as an alternative)

- 500g strong bread flour (it is important to use a stronger flour than normal as you need the extra strength in the gluten to produce strong, pliable pastry)
- 120g lard or white shortening
- 125g Cornish butter
- 1 tsp salt
- 175ml cold water

FILLING:

- 450g good quality beef skirt, cut into cubes
- 450g potato, diced
- 250g swede, diced
- 200g onion, sliced
- Salt & pepper to taste (2:1 ratio)
- Beaten egg and/or milk, to brush

1 Rub the two types of fat lightly into flour until it resembles breadcrumbs.
2 Add water, bring the mixture together and knead until the pastry becomes elastic. This will take longer than normal pastry but it gives the pastry the strength that is needed to hold the filling and retain a good shape. This can also be done in a food mixer.
3 Cover with cling film and leave to rest for 3 hours in the fridge. This is a very important stage as it is almost impossible to roll and shape the pastry when fresh.
4 Roll out the pastry and cut into circles approximately 20cm diameter. A side plate is an ideal size to use as a guide.
5 Layer the vegetables and meat on top of the pastry, adding plenty of seasoning.
6 Bring the pastry around and crimp the edges together (see our guide to crimping, opposite).
7 Glaze with beaten egg or an egg and milk mixture.
8 Bake at 165°C (fan oven) for about 40 – 45 minutes until golden.

TOP TIPS:

- Beef skirt is the cut traditionally used for Cornish pasties. This is the underside of the belly of the animal. It has no fat or gristle, cooks in the same amount of time as the raw vegetables and its juice produces wonderful gravy.
- Use a firm waxy potato such as Maris Peer or Wilja. A floury potato will disintegrate on cooking.

SO, WHAT EXACTLY ARE YOU LOOKING FOR WHEN IN SEARCH OF A GENUINE CORNISH PASTY?

- A genuine Cornish pasty has a distinctive 'D' shape and is crimped on one side, never on top.
- The texture of the filling is chunky, made up of uncooked minced or roughly cut chunks of beef (not less than 12½%), swede, potato, onion with a light seasoning.
- The pastry casing is golden in colour, savoury, glazed with milk or egg and robust enough to retain its shape throughout the cooking and cooling process without splitting or cracking.
- The pasty is slow-baked and no artificial flavourings or additives are used.
- If it's going to be sold as a Cornish pasty, it must, of course, be made in Cornwall.

HOW TO CRIMP

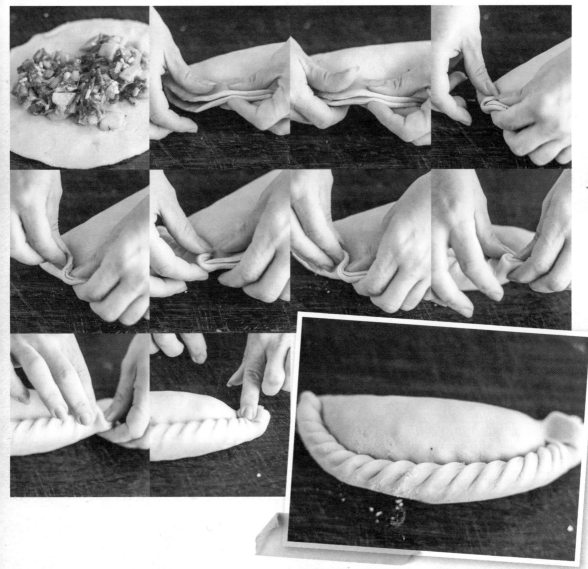

CRIMPING IS ONE OF THE SECRETS TO A TRUE CORNISH PASTY AND A GOOD HAND CRIMP IS USUALLY A SIGN OF A GOOD HANDMADE PASTY – THE NUMBER OF CRIMPS WILL VARY FROM PASTY TO PASTY. WARREN'S BAKERY ARE RENOWNED FOR THEIR TRADITIONAL HAND-CRIMPED PASTIES; HERE ARE THEIR TIPS.

- Lightly brush the edge of the pastry with water.
- Fold the other half of pastry over the filling and squeeze the half circle edges firmly together.
- Push down on the edge of the pasty and, using your index finger and thumb, twist the edge of the pastry over to form a crimp.
- Repeat this process along the edge of the pasty.
- When you've crimped along the edge, tuck the end corners underneath.

If a pasty is crimped by a left-hander it is called a 'cock pasty'. A right-hander makes it a 'hen pasty'.

CORNISH CALENDAR

When Vicki Crwys-Williams moved to St Agnes in 2012 to set up the Cornish Pizza Co with husband John, they knew Cornwall would offer amazing ingredients to top their signature pizza dough, but one of their biggest bugbears was not being able to find out easily when ingredients were in season. The list of ingredients is long and the seasons tend to come early in Cornwall, so it's not always straightforward. As a result of her endeavours to find the answers, Vicki has put together her own list and shares this regularly through a column in the village news.

SPRING, MARCH – MAY

Tasty leafy greens are nature's way of kick-starting your system after winter. Curly kale, broccoli and purple sprouting broccoli, spring greens, spinach, rocket and new season asparagus, early potatoes, spring onions and rhubarb. Locally caugh flat fish such as plaice, turbot, lemon sole, and brill as well as Cornish spring lam The start of salads, watercress and herbs such as basil, sorrel, chives and dill. A rainbow of local primroses. Hot cross buns.

RICHARD AUSTIN

BOB BERRY

SUMMER, JUNE – AUGUST

Strawberries and other soft fruits such as loganberries, gooseberries, raspberries and red, white and blackcurrants. A final week of asparagus, savoy and sweetheart cabbage, bunched baby carrots, broad and French beans, fresh peas, turnips, globe artichokes, fennel, courgette, summer beetroot and mangetout. Try fresh nasturtium flowers for colour and a nice peppery taste in your next salad. Stunning local seafood of lobster, crab, sardines and mackerel.

AUTUMN, SEPTEMBER – NOVEMBER

Squid, red mullet, mussels, native oysters, winkles, razor clams, scallops and skate. Apples, Kea plums, damsons, blackberries and pears. Field mushrooms, squashes and pumpkins, red cabbage, Jerusalem artichokes, swede, parsnips. Game such as wild duck, pheasant. Quince and nuts such as hazel, cob nuts and walnuts.

WINTER, DECEMBER – FEBRUARY

Cod, pollack, fresh clams, local shrimps, and mussels, cabbage, cauliflower, winter kale and greens, swede, parsnip, sprouts and leeks. Venison and goose. Chestnuts to roast.

TIME FOR TEA

Here's a lovely Cornish tea time treat, Tregothnan tea with a Cornish Fairing, the perfect accompaniment.

SELLING TEA TO CHINA. AN UNLIKELY BUT TRUE CORNISH TALE

It was all the ingenious idea of Jonathon Jones, garden director at the Tregothnan estate on the banks of the river Fal, who deduced that since Cornwall provided ideal growing conditions for ornamental camellias, it must surely also be a good place to grow Camellia sinensis, aka tea. He was right, and tea harvesting began at Tregothnan in 2005, making it the first commercial English tea plantation ever and sparking interest from around the globe, including – yes – China.

The estate now produces 35 different types of tea. Standards such as English Breakfast and Earl Grey are perennially popular but the more specialist varieties are finding favour with the new breed of connoisseur leading the tea shop revival on the high street. Look out for the Afternoon Tea blend (drunk black) and the herbals and tisanes made from plants grown on the estate in Cornwall, including the New Zealand native Manuka.

FURNISS/PROPER CORNISH

CORNISH FAIRINGS, THE PERFECT DUNK!

Cornish Fairings are thought to be the oldest Cornish teatime treats, traditionally sold at medieval country fairs (hence the name) and used as love tokens: young men would buy fairings to take home to their sweethearts and families.

Derived from gingerbread, fairings would have been flavoured with luxurious spices and sweeteners such as honey and decorated with almonds or gold leaf. Some of these exotic ingredients were made readily available to Cornwall as a result of sea trade and would have been a welcome treat from the everyday Cornish diet.

Furniss of Redruth were the first manufacturers of fairings on a commercial scale. They have been baking biscuits since 1886 and are the only bakery that can sell Original Cornish Fairings, now a trade-marked name. At the heart of the business is the 60-year-old oven which is the reason why the biscuits have their signature slightly wonky home-made appearance. At 115 feet long, the Furniss Baker Perkins oven, built in 1950, can make up to 7,000 biscuits an hour and she has remained in operation to this day.

To make an original fairing, dry ingredients such as flour and spices are mixed with butter to resemble breadcrumbs. Sugar and golden syrup are then added before the mixture is shaped into biscuits and cooked at high temperature, making the end result brittle and crunchy, ideal for dunking.

SAFFRON — MORE PRECIOUS THAN GOLD

Saffron is easily the most expensive spice in the world, being more precious, by weight, than gold. Made from the carefully picked and dried stigmas of the Crocus sativus flower, the amber coloured spice has a distinct and delicate flavour and adds a golden colour and a slightly bitter, hay-like fragrance to food. Although no-one knows exactly where it first came from, saffron has been used in food, medicine and textiles for centuries - even Cleopatra was said to be a fan. The precious spice doesn't quite grow on trees though; to make just 500g of dry saffron requires a staggering harvest of 50,000–75,000 flowers. Luckily a little goes a long way.

Its arrival on the Cornish coast is thought to date back to the Phoenician traders who sailed to exchange spices and other goods for the tin from the Cornish mines. Cornwall is the only part of the UK where saffron is used in sweet bakery and saffron cakes and buns remain distinctively Cornish, having been around for generations. Saffron cake is traditionally a characteristic of many local feast days and festivals, particularly in the pockets of Cornwall that were once rich in the tin trade, like Redruth, St Day and Camborne. A strongly Methodist county, every Sunday School would hold an annual Tea Treat where, after parading through the parish, everyone would congregate for tea. Children would each be given a saffron bun reportedly 'as big as a cow pat', as part of the celebrations.

THE BEST WAY TO EAT IT?

A slice of this highly fruity yeasted cake is delicious on its own but, for extra Cornish decadence, try a slice spread with salted butter or lashings of Cornish clotted cream. Also makes an amazing bread and butter pudding.

SAFFRON CAKE

EVERY BAKERY HAS ITS OWN CLOSELY GUARDED RECIPE FOR SAFFRON CAKE, JUST AS IT DOES FOR CORNISH PASTIES, BUT WE MANAGED TO PERSUADE MARION SYMONDS FROM PORTREATH BAKERY TO SHARE HERS.

MAKES 3 LOAVES

- 570g strong flour
- 60g granulated sugar
- 10g salt
- 225g white vegetable fat or lard
- 60g fresh yeast or 30g dried yeast
- 170g currants
- 170g sultanas
- 200ml warm water
- 50ml boiling water
- 1g saffron strands

1 Place the saffron into a bowl and pour over the boiling water, set aside for 1 hour.
2 Place the dry ingredients into a mixing bowl fitted with a hook, add the fat and mix to a crumb.
3 Disperse the yeast in the warm water.
4 Add all liquids into the bowl and mix for 6 minutes on medium speed.
5 Cover with a damp cloth and rest for 40 minutes in a warm place.
6 After 40 minutes add the fruit to the dough and leave for another 20 minutes covered with a damp cloth (mix this on a low speed to prevent the fruit breaking).
7 Leave for a further 20 minutes and then hand mould into desired pieces.
8 Cover with a damp cloth and leave in a warm place until doubled in size.
9 Bake in a preheated oven at 210°C for approximately 25 minutes.

A CORNISH TREAT

Few things are more quintessentially Cornish than a clotted cream tea and it's on the hit list for hundreds of thousands of holidaymakers every year. Although there is undoubtedly something special about eating a clotted cream tea in Cornwall, it's really very easy to recreate one anywhere – but make sure you always use real Cornish clotted cream – any other cream simply won't be the same.

Historically, a Cornish cream tea used the now rare 'splits' – a more bread-like, yeasted version of the scone. There has also been long-running debate with our neighbours across the Tamar about whether the cream should go underneath the jam or on top. It is said that the Devonians put their cream under the jam because they are ashamed of it. Here in Cornwall, it is the crowning glory, ALWAYS on the top!

THERE ARE JUST FOUR ESSENTIAL INGREDIENTS:

- Cornish clotted cream
- Scones or splits
- A very high quality jam, usually strawberry
- Tea

HOW TO SERVE

1 Take a very fresh scone (or split) and cut it through the middle. A very fresh scone should simply pull apart.
2 Top each half first with a spoonful of jam, then with a generous dollop of Cornish clotted cream and your cream tea is ready to be enjoyed - with a cup of hot English, tea of course.

TOP TIPS

- If you have an extra sweet tooth, try Thunder and Lightning – replacing the jam with treacle or golden syrup.
- If you're the opposite and don't like your jam too sweet, try using Kea plum jam instead of strawberry jam. Kea plums are a little like damsons, unique to an area of Cornwall beside the Fal estuary, so close in fact that the plums sometimes have to be harvested by shaking them from the trees into a boat.

SPLITS OR SCONES?

Scones are supposed to be quicker and easier to make than splits, which need to be left to rise, but it's surprisingly difficult to make a really good light scone.

CORNISH SPLITS

Splits are so rarely made now, recipes are hard to find. The Chough Bakery in Padstow share theirs, which produces a genuine result, complete with a dusting of icing sugar. Don't be tempted to make the splits too big – your cream tea will fall apart when you bite into it!

MAKES 15 SPLITS

For stage one:

- 160g strong plain flour
- 25g fresh yeast
- 250g tepid water (not hot)
- 25g sugar

For stage two:

- 360g strong plain flour
- 60g sugar
- 15g milk powder
- 70g Cornish butter
- A pinch of salt

This recipe uses a slow developing yeast and gets the yeast started in a 'sponge' to counteract the sugar in the recipe.

Stage one:

1 Dissolve the yeast and sugar in the water.
2 Pour into the flour and whisk.
3 Cover and leave in a warm place.
4 This will ferment and rapidly double in size.
5 When the yeast runs out of sugar, it will begin to collapse.

Stage two:

6 Mix the dry ingredients and then mix in the fat slowly.
7 Add the fermented mixture from stage one slowly until absorbed.
8 Increase the mixer speed until the dough clears and becomes glossy.
9 Cover and leave for about ½ an hour.
10 Knead the dough and then divide into 15 equal pieces and mould into balls.
11 Place on a greased baking tray. Cover and leave until they have doubled their size.
12 Cook in a hot oven 180°C for about 16 minutes.
13 Test to see if they sound hollow.
14 Put on a cooling tray and dredge with icing sugar.
15 See how long you can wait before eating one.

CAFÉ CULTURE

When café culture hit Britain, the big names on the high street were slow to show an interest in sleepy Cornwall. But that didn't mean café culture passed Cornwall by, it gave rise to a fantastically diverse range of independent cafés that could flourish in true Cornish 'go with the flow' style. Cornish café culture is also where the traditional and the contemporary merge seamlessly together. In towns and villages on the coast and in the countryside, you'll find places where you can enjoy full Cornish après-surf fry ups and clotted cream teas alongside coffee to satisfy the most demanding aficionado and menus with refreshing influences from global cuisines.

Apple Tree Café at Sennen, tucked away just half a mile from Land's End.

MIKE NEWMAN

MIKE NEWMAN

BAKED MISS MUFFET WITH HONEY AND ALMONDS

This is one of the quickest and tastiest recipes ever, perfect for lunch or a light supper. It's the epitome of Cornish café culture – creative without fuss, using quality ingredients and letting them speak for themselves.

The idea for the recipe came from local cheese specialist Thomas Hanson and it's on the menu at the Duchy of Cornwall Nursery Café, which you'll find in stunning countryside near Lostwithiel, a beautiful eco building created using traditional natural materials, a project overseen by HRH Prince Charles himself.

Miss Muffet cheese is hand-made near Bude and is deliciously nutty with a little sweetness to it. The almonds and honey enhance those qualities perfectly.

1 Simply take half a Miss Muffet cheese per person, keeping the rind on.
2 Place on a baking sheet or heatproof dish, cut side up.
3 Drizzle with good quality Cornish runny honey and sprinkle toasted almonds on the top.
4 Pop in the top of a hot oven for no more than 5 minutes and serve with crusty bread and perhaps a simple green salad.

all you need is
COFFEE

HOW TO MAKE THE PERFECT COFFEE
ORIGIN FOUNDER TOM SOBEY
SPILLS THE ROASTED BEANS.

ESSENTIAL KIT
- French press (cafetière)
- Hand grinder
- Scales
- Fresh coffee beans (no more than 2 weeks from roast date)
- Timer (use smart phone to tweet progress...)

METHOD
1 Place French press onto the scales and fill with cool water. Calculate how much water, in grams, the press holds.
2 To brew excellent coffee at home you need to use a ratio of 80g of coffee per litre of water used. (Maths tip: 500g = 500ml of water, therefore for 500ml of water use 40g fresh coffee).
3 Boil fresh filtered water and allow to cool for 30 seconds.
4 Weigh correct amount of coffee into the grinder and grind to the consistency of rough sand.
5 Pour into the French press.
6 Pour the water on top of the ground coffee and start the timer.
7 After 2 minutes agitate the coffee by stirring in a circular motion.
8 After 4 minutes plunge the French press, and pour.
9 Drink black to fully appreciate the subtlety of the flavour.

NADIA PENDLETON, HALF ITALIAN AND NOW LIVING IN CORNWALL, MAKES FANTASTIC BISCOTTI BASED ON HER FAMILY'S TRADITIONAL RECIPES BUT GIVING THEM A CORNISH TWIST. A DELICIOUS FUSION OF CORNISH AND ITALIAN TRADITIONS, AND THE PERFECT ACCOMPANIMENT TO ANY CUP OF GOOD COFFEE.

NADIA'S ORANGE, CRANBERRY & ALMOND BISCOTTI

- 2 large Cornish free range eggs
- 2 tbsp orange marmalade
- 5g Cornish sea salt
- 60ml light olive oil
- 150g caster sugar
- 10ml vanilla extract
- 4-5 strands saffron
- 220g plain flour
- 5g baking powder
- 190g whole almonds, roughly chopped
- 60g dried cranberries

1 Preheat oven to 150°C.
2 In a bowl or food processor, blend the oil and the sugar, then mix in the vanilla and beat in the eggs. Add the strands of saffron, stir and allow the mix to steep for 5 minutes.
3 In a separate bowl, combine the flour, salt and baking powder.
4 Gradually stir in the egg mixture, then fold in the marmalade, cranberries and nuts.
5 Line a baking tray with greaseproof paper. Divide the mix into two halves and, using wet hands, form two long logs. The dough will be sticky.
6 Bake for 35 minutes or until light brown. Remove from the oven and allow to cool for 10 minutes.
7 Reduce the oven to 135°C.
8 Slice the logs on the diagonal to about ¾ inch thick. Lay them on their sides and bake for 8-10 minutes or until dry.

MINI MORSELS

STREET FOOD, TAPAS, ANTIPASTI, SHARING PLATTERS, LITTLE
PLATES... THE MOOD FOR FOOD THESE DAYS IS RELAXED,
UNPRETENTIOUS, FLEXIBLE AND ALL ABOUT FRIENDS, AND
THAT'S JUST HOW WE LIKE IT HERE IN CORNWALL.

"Working in our kitchen can be
a challenge as our dishes will
often be on for just a day and
then we're on to something
else. We like to respond to
what's in the ground and sea
otherwise we'd have to buy it
out of Cornwall and that's
not what we're about. We have
Cornish potatoes dug up in the
morning and on the menu in
the evening, that's how we like
to work."

At Jamie Oliver's Fifteen Cornwall, whiling away the evening with friends, grazing on antipasti around the sharing table and watching the sun drop behind the Atlantic horizon, is about as chilled as it gets. This is a little taste of Italy on the north coast of Cornwall, giving local produce an Italian vibe, à la Jamie. Head chef Andy Appleton shares a few of his suggestions to help you recreate this relaxed style at home.

CORNISH CRAB STUFFED ZUCCHINI FLOWERS WITH AGRETTI

Crab is great in this dish but here but the options are endless. Soft cheeses like Cornish goats cheese are good with peas and mint. Simply stuff the flowers with your chosen mix and deep fry in a light tempura. Serve with Agretti, a Mediterranean vegetable that tastes a bit like spinach and loves coastal climes like Cornwall.

ARANCHINI WITH CORNISH BLUE CHEESE AND TARRAGON AIOLI

Aranchini, or risotto balls, are very popular as street food in Italy. You need a good strong cheese to go with the rice, so Cornish Blue, which melts in the mouth when you bite into it, is perfect. For the aioli you could use any herb or wild garlic added to a good mayonnaise.

CHARGRILLED ST ENODOC ASPARAGUS WITH DELI FARM COPPA HAM

One of the easiest little dishes in the world! Simply wrap coppa ham around the asparagus spears and chargrill them from raw, retaining a nice crunch. Treat them like breadsticks and dip them in good oil or aioli.

DID YOU KNOW?

The Cornwall Foundation of Promise, which owns Jamie Oliver's Fifteen Cornwall, is a charity that gives hope and promise to young people who've not had the best start in life. It has enrolled more than 120 apprentice chefs since the restaurant opened in 2006 and more than 70% are still cheffing today.

SOUTH SIDE STORY

IN FOODIE TERMS CORNWALL'S SOUTH COAST HAS LIVED IN THE SHADOW OF ITS LIMELIGHT-HUGGING NORTH COAST BROTHER FOR YEARS AS PADSTOW'S GOURMET REPUTATION FILTERED OUT TO ROCK AND BEYOND. BUT NOT ANY MORE. FROM DOWNDERRY TO MOUSEHOLE THE SOUTH IS COOL AGAIN AND ONCE MORE IT'S ALL DOWN TO THE FOOD. NOWHERE IS THAT MORE APPARENT THAN AROUND PORTSCATHO ON THE ROSELAND, WHERE AN ENERGETIC CLUSTER INCLUDING MICHELIN STARS AND BEACHSIDE BARS, IS PROVING THAT, FOR THOSE IN THE KNOW, THIS IS WHERE IT'S AT. THE QUIET ONE HAS STARTED TO ROAR!

ROAST BREAST AND CRISPY LEG OF CORNISH DUCK WITH CARDAMOM & CARROT PURÉE

Tim Pile is head chef at the Rosevine, a big house by the sea near Portscatho – hotel, holiday home and restaurant in one.

SERVES 4

- 4 Cornish duck breasts
- 6 duck legs
- Duck fat
- Cornish sea salt and spices and aromatics (eg cinnamon, thyme, garlic, orange zest)
- 6 carrots
- 4 cardamom pods
- 70g Cornish butter
- Panko breadcrumbs
- 1 cup plain flour
- 1 egg and a splash of milk (egg wash)

1 Rub the duck legs generously with the salt, spices and aromatics. Leave uncovered in the fridge for 24 hours.

2 Wash the duck legs under cold running water, put in a deep roasting tin and cover with duck fat. Place covered in the oven at 140°C for approximately 2½ hours. Remove from oven and allow to cool. Pull the meat from the bones and lay on a double sheet of cling film. Roll in the cling film to form a ballotine (thick sausage shape – approximately 5cm diameter). Twist or tie the ends up tightly and refrigerate to set.

3 Peel and dice the carrots. Melt the butter in a pan and lightly sweat the carrots, adding the whole cardamom pods. Add a splash of stock or water and cook until soft. Season with salt and blend to a smooth purée.

5 Score the skin on the duck breasts and season. Heat a splash of oil in a metal-handled frying pan. Place breasts skin side down for 5 minutes. Place the whole pan in the oven at 190°C for 5 minutes. Take pan from oven and turn the meat over, leaving off the heat in the pan to finish cooking through.

7 Remove the cling film from the leg ballotine and cut into equal sized portions (approximately 2cm wide). Coat each portion with flour, egg and breadcrumbs and lightly fry.

8 Slice the duck breasts and serve each portion with the purée and sliced confit leg.

A mixture of roasted root vegetables and a red wine sauce would suit this dish on a winter evening.

Cornish Feasts & Festivals

Anyone familiar with the Cornish will know they are not averse to a celebration or two. At one time virtually every Cornish parish would have had its own annual celebration, usually known as a feast day, and often related to its patronal saint. Over the centuries, other community events have evolved, celebrating famous people or traditions, often associated with tin mining or farming. Each represents a piece of Cornish history and heritage and in all of them one thing is guaranteed - food and drink will be an important part of the proceedings.

CORNISH CELEBRATIONS
TOP PICKS

Rock Oyster Festival.

5TH MARCH

ST PIRAN'S DAY

Often thought of as the Patron Saint of Cornwall but in fact the Patron Saint of Tinners, St Piran's Day is to Cornwall what St David's Day is to Wales and St Patrick's Day is to Ireland.

APRIL

TREVITHICK DAY, CAMBORNE

Paying homage to the town's father of steam, Richard Trevithick, including a parade of steam engines.

1ST MAY

'OBBY 'OSS DAY, PADSTOW

The day is thought to stem from Pagan origins and celebrates the start of summer with singing and dancing and the parading of a red 'Oss and a blue 'Oss in the streets.

8TH MAY

FLORA DAY, HELSTON

Starting at 7am, the dancing to the traditional tune of the Furry Dance goes on all day, but the thump of the big bass drum that signals the start of the midday dance is the moment everyone waits for.

JUNE

ROYAL CORNWALL SHOW, WADEBRIDGE

One of the best county shows anywhere, retaining and proudly showing off its roots with farming.

MURDOCH DAY, REDRUTH

A celebration of Redruth's famous resident engineer, credited with inventing the gaslight

GOLOWAN AND MAZEY DAY, PENZANCE

Golowan is Cornish for midsummer and originally involved parading lighted tar barrels around the town until it was outlawed due to rising insurance premiums! Revived in 1991 it is now a cultural celebration culminating in Mazey Day, with a parade and much activity in Penzance.

JULY

LAFROWDA DAY, ST JUST

Lafrowda Day is a community celebration, with a colourful procession through the town, along with music traditional and new.

Padstow Christmas Festival.

FOOD FESTIVALS

The love of the food festival concept hasn't escaped Cornwall either – and why would it when there is so much to celebrate? Many have become a firm diary date with people from near and far. Above all, any festival is a chance for people to relax and sup with friends. At all of Cornwall's major food festivals you can do just that, while checking out who's who and what's what in the Cornish food world.

A YEAR IN CORNISH FOOD FESTIVALS

Cornwall Food and Drink Festival.

APRIL

PORTHLEVEN FOOD AND MUSIC FESTIVAL

Kicking off the Cornish food festival season, a wonderful day of food and music in this pretty fishing village.

MAY

CORNWALL ASPARAGUS FESTIVAL

Paying homage to the ingredient that heralds the spring.

JUNE

ROCK OYSTER FESTIVAL

The hip and happenin' food and music festival.

LOOE FESTIVAL OF FOOD AND DRINK

This oft forgotten corner of South East Cornwall celebrates its fast developing reputation for great eating and drinking.

AUGUST

NEWLYN FISH FESTIVAL

Cornwall's largest celebration of the fruits of the sea.

SEPTEMBER

CORNWALL FOOD & DRINK FESTIVAL, TRURO

Quite simply the biggest celebration of Cornish food and drink anywhere.

OCTOBER

FALMOUTH OYSTER FESTIVAL

Signalling the start of the oyster season – sailing, shucking, eating, drinking.

BOSCASTLE FOOD AND ARTS FESTIVAL

Started as a means of helping the village overcome the disastrous floods in 2004, this festival has grown to become one of Cornwall's gems.

DECEMBER

PADSTOW CHRISTMAS FESTIVAL

The season ends fittingly in the town that has done more for Cornish food than any other.

PRIDE OF CORNWALL

Cornwall Food & Drink Members

FROM FLEDGLING IDEAS TO NAMES KNOWN AND LOVED AROUND THE GLOBE, WE'RE HONOURED TO WORK WITH A FANTASTIC RANGE OF EXCELLENT PEOPLE AND PRODUCTS. TAKE YOUR PICK OF ANY OF OUR MEMBERS AND WE'RE PRETTY SURE YOU WON'T BE DISAPPOINTED.

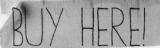

BUY HERE!

Baker Tom's Bread
POOL, FALMOUTH AND TRURO
Fresh speciality breads, pastries and cakes baked daily, using traditional methods and the finest organic and local ingredients.
www.bakertom.co.uk

Banbury's Turkeys
NR WADEBRIDGE
Christmas turkeys with a difference - happy, healthy and hand-reared on a family farm on the north Cornish coast.
www.banburysturkeys.co.uk

Breakfast Book
PADSTOW
A range of nutritious, high quality granolas and mueslis. Four lines available, including a gluten-free variety.
www.breakfastbook.co.uk

Brian Etherington Meat Company
SCORRIER
Farm shop, butchery academy and catering butchers supplying Cornwall, Devon and the Isles of Scilly.
www.etherington-meats.co.uk

Buttermilk Confections
WADEBRIDGE
One of the oldest fudge producers in Cornwall making national award-winning confectionery.
www.buttermilkconfections.co.uk

Callestick Farm Ice Cream
NR TRURO
Quality ice cream using fresh milk, 100% natural ingredients and the farm's own spring water. Available in 30 different flavours.
www.callestickfarm.co.uk

Camel Valley
NANSTALLON
Producing award-winning, world-class wines in a beautiful corner of Cornwall since 1989.
www.camelvalley.com

Chough Bakery
PADSTOW
A small, family-run bakery, famed for its award-winning pasties - filled and crimped by hand. Speciality breads and confectionery. Mail order available.
www.thechoughbakery.co.uk

Clare's Cottage Bread & Cakes
BISSOE
A range of breads and cakes from a cottage kitchen. Available at the Pandora Inn and the Punchbowl and Ladle.
01872 864822

Cornish Cheese Company
NR LISKEARD
Home of Cornish Blue Cheese, handmade on the farm. Awarded 'Best Cheese in the World' in 2010.
www.cornishcheese.co.uk

Cornish Country Meats
LISKEARD
Proud to sell home and locally produced meat as well as more exotic meats, plus a range of pasties and pies.
www.cornishcountrymeats.co.uk

Cornish Food Box Company
TRURO
Delivering boxes of fresh, seasonal 100% Cornish food and drink to homes, offices and holiday cottages. Making it easy for local people to buy local food.
www.thecornishfoodboxcompany.co.uk

Cornish Gin Distillery
ST COLUMB
Producer of hand-crafted artisan Cornish Gin, distilled in Cornwall with Cornish spring water in a traditional copper pot still.
www.cornishgin.com

Cornish Meadow Preserves
NR HELSTON
An award-winning family business, producing bespoke and traditionally made preserves and mustards.
www.cornishmeadow.co.uk

Cornish Orchards
DULOE
Producers of quality Cornish cider, alcoholic ginger beer, apple juice and soft drinks using freshly pressed juice and the best traditional cider making practices.
www.cornishorchards.co.uk

Cornish Premier Pasties
ST COLUMB
Manufacturers of quality pasties, traditional and speciality, using fresh ingredients, sourced as locally as possible. Suppliers to wholesale and retail customers countrywide.
www.cornishpremierpasties.co.uk

Cornish Sea Salt
HELSTON
Hand-harvested on the Lizard Peninsula from the clearest waters. Flavoured pinch salts also available.
www.cornishseasalt.co.uk

Cornish Venison Company
NEWQUAY
Venison and game products, locally harvested and produced, rich in flavour and taken from the wild following UK best practice guidelines.
07988 323410

Cornishfoodmarket.co.uk
FALMOUTH
A unique, online food shopping service delivering locally-sourced meat, fish, dairy, bread, fruit and vegetables to homes around Cornwall.
www.cornishfoodmarket.co.uk

Davidstow Cheddar
CAMELFORD
Making Cornish Cheddar for 60 years; a combination of knowledge, skill and patience make the award-winning range unique, creamy and delicious.
www.davidstowcheddar.co.uk

Deli Farm Charcuterie
DELABOLE
Artisan producers of award-winning air-dried charcuterie, made with prime cuts of locally sourced meat.
www.delifarmcharcuterie.co.uk

Doble Quality Foods
ST AGNES
Suppliers of chilled, ambient and frozen goods to the catering trade in Cornwall and Devon.
www.doblefoods.co.uk

Furniss
NR REDRUTH
A proud old Cornish biscuit brand that is particularly renowned for its famous Cornish Fairings.
www.furniss-foods.co.uk

Grumpies
LAUNCESTON
Seriously good hand-made pies made with Cornish meats, cheeses, beer and cider.
www.grumpiesofcornwall.co.uk

Hands-On Coffee Roasters
WADEBRIDGE
Great tasting coffee roasted in-house by this environmentally friendly company.
www.hands-on-coffee.co.uk

Harbour Brewing Company
BODMIN
A small craft brewery committed to making contemporary beers with uncompromising taste.
www.harbourbrewing.com

Healthy Boxes
PENZANCE
A West Cornwall veg box scheme delivering specially selected, fresh produce to those focused on sourcing their ingredients locally.
www.healthyboxes.co.uk

Ideal Foods
LISKEARD
Seafood traders, focused on international export. Their motto: 'If it swims we can supply it'.
www.ideal-foods.co.uk

Isles of Scilly Farmers' and Growers' Initiative
ST. MARY'S
Dedicated to promoting and enhancing food producers and the agricultural industry on one of the smallest island communities in the UK.
www.farmscilly.co.uk

Just Water
BODMIN
Still and sparkling spring water, bottled at source on their farm near Bodmin and delivered throughout Cornwall and Devon.
www.justwater.biz

Keltek Brewery
REDRUTH
A purpose built brewery, brewing award-winning real ales including King, Magik, Golden Lance and Even Keel.
www.keltekbrewery.co.uk

Kernow Sausage Company
TREGONY
A family owned and run business with a range of sausages and bacon that have become popular with Michelin starred chefs, local businesses and families alike.
www.kernowsausages.com

Kittow's Butchers
PAR
Fifth generation family butchers and deli based in Fowey since 1880. Quality and animal welfare are of the utmost importance.
www.kittowsbutchers.co.uk

Knightor Winery & Restaurant
NR ST AUSTELL
Located above St Austell Bay near the Eden Project. Still and sparkling wines produced from grapes of their own vineyards in South Cornwall.
www.knightor.com

Lynher Dairies
PONSANOOTH
Makers of handmade Cornish Yarg in open vats on the farm in West Cornwall.
www.lynherdairies.co.uk

Nadia's Biscotti
PADSTOW
Hand-made Italian style biscuits based on a traditional family recipe and made using high quality, local ingredients.
www.nadiasbiscotti.com

Nancarrow Organic Farm
NR TRURO
A family business of over 200 years, producing delicious organic meat, reared outdoors to the highest standards of animal welfare. Available direct from the farm.
www.nancarrowfarm.co.uk

Nicky Grant Cakes & Chocolate
NR HAYLE
An award-winning chocolatier, using some of the best local ingredients to produce handmade chocolates, wedding cakes and favours.
www.nickygrant.com

Ninemaidens Mead
LANNER
Producing a range of quality meads since 1999, carefully made with the finest honey from their own hives.
www.ninemaidensmead.com

Origin Coffee
HELSTON
Crafting speciality filter & espresso coffee and working hard to make sure every bean roasted is as perfect as they can get it.
www.origincoffee.co.uk

Padstow Christmas Festival
PADSTOW
A seasonal celebration of local food, drink, Christmas shopping, music, arts and entertainment.
www.padstowchristmasfestival.co.uk

Penpont Brewery
ALTARNUN
Using their own Cornish spring water, blended with the finest raw ingredients to produce a variety of real ales in casks and bottles.
www.penpontbrewery.co.uk

Philip Warren & Son
LAUNCESTON
Graziers and exceptional craft butchers.
www.philipwarrenbutchers.co.uk

Polgoon Vineyard & Orchard
PENZANCE
An award-winning producer of Cornish wines, cider and fruit juices.
www.polgoon.co.uk

Portreath Bakery
PORTREATH
Freshly baked pasties, other savouries, bread, confectionery, wedding and other celebration cakes. Catering for all occasions and bakery workshops for schools and individuals.
www.portreathbakery.co.uk

Primrose Herd
NR REDRUTH
Pedigree pig breeders producing award-winning sausages, bacon, hog's pudding and pork products for retail and wholesale customers.
www.primroseherd.co.uk

Proper Cornish
BODMIN
Handmade Cornish pasties done the proper way, supplied to wholesalers, independent retailers, supermarkets, catering outlets and tourist attractions across the UK and beyond.
www.propercornish.co.uk

Rebel Brewing Company
PENRYN
A microbrewery producing fine traditional ales as well as unique and interesting world beers in a sustainable and conscientious way.
www.rebelbrewing.co.uk

Riverford Home Delivery
BODMIN
Delivering organic foods, including fresh produce from Cornish farms, around the county.
www.riverford.co.uk

Riviera Produce
NR HAYLE
Supplier of fresh produce direct to retail customers from their purpose built facility.
www.rivieraproduce.eu

Rodda's Creamery
SCORRIER
Producing their famous clotted cream since 1890, Rodda's also use their milk for butter, pouring cream, fudge, shortbread and crème fraîche.
www.roddas.co.uk

Rowe's Cornish Bakers
PENRYN
Baking sweet and savoury treats for over 60 years, including Cornish pasties, cakes and scones, using local ingredients and traditional methods. Outlets throughout Cornwall.
www.rowesbakers.co.uk

Sharp's Brewery
ROCK
Modern brewer of cask beer, the largest in the South West. Brewer of Doom Bar, one of the UK's fastest growing beers.
www.sharpsbrewery.co.uk

Simply Oils
NR NEWQUAY

Oil produced from rapeseed grown on the fertile soils of the North Cornish coast. A perfect partner for all cooking.

www.simply-oils.com

Skinner's Brewery
TRURO

A multi-award-winning range of ales and lager - including the famous Betty Stogs, Queen of Cornish ales.

www.skinnersbrewery.com

St Austell Brewery
ST AUSTELL

Brewing beer and real ale in Cornwall since 1851, with over 170 pubs in the South West. Beers include award-winning bottled and cask ales such as Tribute and Proper Job.

www.staustellbrewery.co.uk

St Ewe Free Range Eggs
TREGONY

Hand-collected, free-range eggs, available in shops, supermarkets and from the farm.

www.stewe.co.uk

Tamblyn's
SALTASH

A family business boasting complete control over the quality of the pork reared for their sausages, resulting in a high percentage of premium pork meat.

www.tamblyns.co.uk

Tregothnan
NR TRURO

England's first and only tea producer, this working estate is internationally known for its fine products.

www.tregothnan.co.uk

Treleaven's Luxury Cornish Ice Cream
EAST LOOE

Luxury ice cream, handmade to a traditional Italian recipe using only the finest ingredients. Over 90 flavours.

www.treleavens.co.uk

Trenance Chocolate
NR HELSTON

Luxury chocolate products made in Mullion. Buy at their shop, in other outlets across Cornwall and online.

www.trenancechocolate.co.uk

Trewithen Dairy
LOSTWITHIEL

A family-run dairy producing milk, clotted cream, butter, yogurt, crème fraîche and buttermilk - supplying retailers, caterers, wholesalers and processors throughout Cornwall and beyond.

www.trewithendairy.co.uk

Truro Farmers' Market
TRURO

A collection of Cornwall's finest food producers trading in Truro every Wednesday and Saturday, and in Falmouth every Tuesday.

www.trurofarmersmarket.co.uk

Warren's Bakery
ST JUST

Dedicated to creating delicious, innovative and traditional bakery products, using locally-sourced ingredients and working with local partners.

www.warrensbakery.co.uk

Wing of St Mawes
INDIAN QUEENS

Fresh seafood and shellfish for restaurants and hotels throughout the South West. Household deliveries available throughout the UK via the Cornish Fishmonger.

www.wingofstmawes.co.uk

EAT HERE!

Alverton Hotel
TRURO

A magnificent four star, Grade II listed hotel, with an award-winning restaurant, bar, function rooms, relaxed terrace and private gardens.

www.thealverton.co.uk

Apple Tree Café
SENNEN

A welcoming community café, bakery and arts studio near Land's End. Serving breakfasts, homemade bread, fresh salads, fish specials and cream teas all year round.

www.theappletreecafe.co.uk

Archie Browns
PENZANCE AND TRURO

Vegetarian café and health food shop. Open Monday to Saturday serving breakfast, lunch and afternoon tea.

www.archiebrowns.co.uk

Atlantic Hotel
ST MARY'S, ISLES OF SCILLY

Located in the heart of St Mary's, this hotel and restaurant combines great hospitality with all the amenities of a full service hotel.

www.atlantichotelscilly.co.uk

Atlantic Inn
ST. MARY'S, ISLES OF SCILLY

Overlooking the harbour, the perfect place to relax and enjoy the stunning scenery of the Isles of Scilly.

www.staustellbrewery.co.uk

Barclay House
LOOE

Two AA rosette restaurant with stunning river views, using the very best locally sourced ingredients.

www.barclayhouse.co.uk

Ben's Cornish Kitchen
MARAZION

Voted Best Restaurant in the South West at the 2013 Food Magazine Reader Awards. A chilled out place to eat.

www.benscornishkitchen.com

Blue Plate
DOWNDERRY

'Food for any mood' featuring the area's finest, freshest produce lovingly prepared and simply presented.

www.blueplatecornwall.com

Blue Tomato Café
ROCK

A unique beachside café with gorgeous views over the Camel Estuary, offering locally sourced food and drink.

www.bluetomatocafe.co.uk

Boscastle Farm Shop & Café
BOSCASTLE

Surrounded by National Trust Farmland and less than 50 yards to the South West Coast Path, the views are breath-taking. Passionate about local produce.

www.boscastlefarmshop.co.uk

Café Roseland
ST MAWES

A bright, fresh café serving quality, homemade food in a seaside location. Also catering for events.

www.merrittsimplyhomemade.co.uk

Castle Restaurant
BUDE

AA rosette restaurant with views over Summerleaze beach. Relaxed and informal, offering superb modern European dining. Wedding and outdoor catering available.

www.thecastlerestaurantbude.co.uk

Central Inn
NEWQUAY

Located in the heart of Newquay, perfect for a leisurely coffee, early evening cocktail or a relaxed meal with friends.

www.thecentralnewquay.co.uk

Cornish Pizza Company
ST AGNES

Thin crust pizzas made using dough made daily on the premises, hand-stretched to order with fresh, locally sourced toppings. Take away available.

www.thecornishpizzacompany.co.uk

Cornwall Catering Excellence
ST AGNES

A collaboration of eight organisations supplying Cornwall's catering industry.

01872 552121

County Arms
TRURO

A place to meet, eat, drink and stay. A bar and restaurant with a large car park, function room and terrace.

www.countyarmstruro.co.uk

Deli Cornwall Café
ST ERTH

A traditional Cornish tearoom with an online shop selling the finest locally sourced Cornish foodstuffs in eco jute hampers.

www.delicornwall.co.uk

Duchy of Cornwall Nursery Café
NR LOSTWITHIEL

Relaxed comfortable café serving food freshly cooked to order. Roaring log fire in winter and an outside terrace for warmer days, with views across the River Fowey Valley to Restormel Castle.

www.duchyofcornwallnursery.co.uk

Eden Project
BODELVA

Watch delicious dishes being created in the Eden Bakery or savour freshly prepared Mediterranean cuisine in the Med Café.

www.edenproject.com

Espressini
FALMOUTH

Artisan espresso bar and coffee shop, sourcing super seasonal speciality coffee and serving local food. Available for private events.

www.espressini.co.uk

Falmouth Packet Inn
ROSUDGEON

Award-winning, family-run pub situated in an area of outstanding beauty and using locally sourced, organic ingredients.

www.falmouthpacketinn.co.uk

Fifteen Cornwall
NR NEWQUAY

Part of a global social enterprise founded by Jamie Oliver, aiming to inspire people through food.

www.fifteencornwall.co.uk

Flying Fish at St Michael's Hotel
FALMOUTH

An award-winning restaurant with views of Falmouth Bay. Stylish, contemporary and friendly with an exciting range of dishes using fresh and seasonal produce.

www.stmichaelshotel.co.uk

Fodders
TRURO

Freshly prepared locally sourced wholefoods including veggie and vegan meals. An espresso bar with locally roasted coffee, home-baked cakes and fresh sandwiches.

www.fodderstruro.co.uk

Fort Inn
NEWQUAY
A family pub, specialising in catering for young children, serving food daily with a large garden overlooking the bay and harbour.
www.fortinnnewquay.co.uk

Godolphin Arms
MARAZION
A family run inn perched on the sea wall opposite the beautiful St Michael's Mount.
www.godolphinarms.co.uk

Great Western Hotel
NEWQUAY
Hotel and pub with sea views, clifftop garden, terrace and only a few steps from the golden sandy beach.
www.greatwesternnewquay.co.uk

Greenbank Hotel
FALMOUTH
This harbour-side restaurant is the perfect place to enjoy the bounty of the South West's waters. Locally sourced seasonal menu prepared by head chef, Fiona Were.
www.greenbank-hotel.co.uk

Harbour Inn
PORTHLEVEN
A lively pub situated on the harbour serving fantastic food all year round using fresh local produce.
www.harbourinnporthleven.co.uk

Headland Hotel
NEWQUAY
Family-owned and run for over 30 years, the hotel prides itself on delivering outstanding service in a world class position.
www.headlandhotel.co.uk

Heather's Coffee Shop
PENDEEN
A small, friendly café serving locally sourced, fresh ingredients in breakfasts, light lunches and homemade cakes. Outside seating.
01736 788069

Heligan Tearoom and Bakery
PENTEWAN
Located in the magical Lost Gardens of Heligan and offering delicious, seasonal home cooked meals served with rustic charm all year round.
www.heligan.com

Holmbush Inn
ST AUSTELL
A lively and friendly pub, with a beer garden and conservatory. Serving a range of St Austell Ales and good home cooked food.
www.holmbushinn.co.uk

Hotel Tresanton
ST MAWES
Diners can enjoy the restaurant's large terrace and the daily changing menu features local meat, seafood and organic vegetables.
www.tresanton.com

Lafafa Catering
GULVAL
Caterers of Middle Eastern cuisine for parties, weddings and business functions.
www.lafafacatering.co.uk

Lifeboat Inn
ST IVES
Traditional harbour-side pub with log fire, wooden beams, granite pillars and outstanding views of the sea.
www.staustellbrewery.co.uk

Melinsey Mill
VERYAN
16th century watermill with café, arts and crafts, rustic shelters, pond walk, historical artefacts and homemade food.
www.melinseymill.co.uk

Nathan Outlaw Restaurants
ROCK
Restaurant Nathan Outlaw boasts two Michelin stars and serves an impressive 8-course dinner tasting menu. The Seafood & Grill offers an à la carte menu, based around market fish and the finest Cornish meat.
www.nathan-outlaw.com

New Yard Restaurant
TRELOWARREN
Locally sourced, fresh, seasonal Cornish ingredients, cooked simply and served in a welcoming atmosphere.
www.newyardrestaurant.co.uk

Norway Inn
PERRANARWORTHAL
A great place to stop for a meal, a drink or to stay. Located between Truro and Falmouth.
www.norwayinn.co.uk

Old Custom House
PADSTOW
One of the finest buildings in Padstow. Famous for its fine food, award-winning ales and elegant accommodation.
www.oldcustomhousepadstow.co.uk

Old Success Inn
SENNEN COVE
Magnificent views overlooking the beach and Whitesand Bay towards The Brisons rocks and Cape Cornwall, the only cape in England.
www.oldsuccess.co.uk

Oliver's
FALMOUTH
A small restaurant, owned and run by Ken and Wendy Symons who are passionate about local produce, prepared and served in a fun, relaxed space.
www.oliversfalmouth.com

Oystercatcher Bar
POLZEATH

A popular bar overlooking one of Cornwall's top surfing beaches, with gardens and patio.

www.oystercatcherpolzeath.co.uk

Pedn-Olva Hotel
ST IVES

Overlooking the ancient town and harbour, an ideal place to stay, dine and relax. Weddings and special events venue.

www.pednolva.co.uk

Penventon Park Hotel
REDRUTH

Luxury hotel with a relaxed yet decadent feel. Dine in the restaurant or pamper yourself in the spa.

www.penventon.com

Picnic Cornwall
FALMOUTH

Independent coffee shop and deli serving exceptional Cornish produce with fantastic customer service. Order online for delivery or collection.

www.picniccornwall.co.uk

Queens Hotel
ST IVES

Listed Georgian hotel in the heart of St Ives offering food at reasonable prices and a perfect pint within relaxed and stylish surroundings.

www.queenshotelstives.com

Rashleigh Arms
CHARLESTOWN

A delightful 4-star gold village inn and restaurant in the heart of Charlestown.

www.rashleigharms.co.uk

Red River Café
POOL

Built around a site of mining heritage, serving fresh, bistro-style food in the relaxed and cosy Old Carpenter's Workshop.

www.heartlandscornwall.com

Rosewarne Manor
NR HAYLE

Awarded two AA rosettes, known for its à la carte, steaks and carvery. A rural setting with large gardens, popular for functions and weddings.

www.rosewarnemanor.co.uk

Scarlet Hotel
MAWGAN PORTH

Local and seasonal food, with daily changing menus created by acclaimed head chef, Tom Hunter.

www.scarlethotel.co.uk

Ship Inn
MOUSEHOLE

A welcoming pub situated in this famous fishing village. Serving local beer and ciders, chilled wines and cockle-warming coffees.

www.shipinnmousehole.co.uk

Shipwright's
PADSTOW

Fresh local produce with a wide selection of salads, main meals and light bites.

www.staustellbrewery.co.uk

South West Lakes Trust
BUDE AND LISKEARD

The region's largest combined environmental and recreational charity. Enjoy outdoor activities and the cafés at Tamar Lake near Bude and Siblyback Lake near Liskeard, which use locally sourced ingredients.

www.swlakestrust.org.uk

St Kew Harvest Farm Shop
WADEBRIDGE

Shop and wholefood café, with wood-fired bread oven and market garden. All foods are grown, baked, produced or sourced according to the seasons, locally and sustainably.

www.stkewharvest.co.uk

The Green Room
NR PADSTOW

Fine dining in a relaxed atmosphere, with gourmet dishes created by head chef and MasterChef 2008 winner James Nathan.

www.retallackresort.com

The Harbour
PORT ISAAC

A cosy, intimate restaurant in a stunning location, nestled at the top of the slipway.

www.theharbourportisaac.com

The Llawnroc Hotel
GORRAN HAVEN

Luxury boutique hotel with a large bistro and terrace with sea views. Serving the best and freshest local produce.

www.thellawnrochotel.co.uk

The Park Café
MAWGAN PORTH

A licensed café with space to enjoy delicious food and have a good time. Open to non-residents.

www.mawganporth.co.uk

The Point
POLZEATH

Breakfast, lunch and dinner specials including daily-landed market fish, all cooked to order by a team of talented chefs.

www.thepointatpolzeath.co.uk

The Port William Inn
TINTAGEL

Located at Trebarwith Strand, a pub and restaurant renowned for excellent food and a comfortable welcoming bar.

www.theportwilliam.co.uk

The Rosevine
NR PORTHSCATHO
The restaurant has a relaxed atmosphere. Dishes are cooked simply with what's in season, using as much local produce as possible, all by the beach.
www.rosevine.co.uk

The Seafood Restaurant
PADSTOW
Rick and Jill Stein have four restaurants in Padstow; The Seafood Restaurant, St Petroc's Bistro, Rick Stein's Café and Stein's Fish & Chips. They have a pub, The Cornish Arms in St Merryn and Rick Stein's Fish in Falmouth.
www.rickstein.com

The Waterfront
POLZEATH
Restaurant and bar with spectacular panoramic views of Polzeath Beach and Pentire Point. Outstanding cuisine sourced locally.
www.waterfrontpolzeath.co.uk

The Weir
BUDE
Contemporary bistro specialising in coffee and breakfast with fresh local food. Overlooking a fishing lake, play area and interactive wildlife centre.
www.weir-restaurant-bude.co.uk

Tides Restaurant at The Mariner's
ROCK
With stunning views of the Camel estuary, head chef Tom Scade savours creating dishes from quality Cornish produce.
www.tidesrock.com

Tolcarne Inn
NEWLYN
A small pub that focuses on providing the best in fresh local seafood, with all the catch coming in from local boats.
www.tolcarneinn.co.uk

Trevathan Farm Shop & Restaurant
PORT ISAAC
Family run café serving home cooked breakfast, lunch, cakes and cream teas. Traditional Sunday lunch with home produced beef and lamb.
www.trevathanfarm.com

Victoria Inn
PERRANUTHNOE
Reputedly one of the oldest inns in Cornwall, serving award-winning food, fine wines, good local ales, ciders and Cornish lager.
www.victoriainn-penzance.co.uk

Watergate Bay Hotel
NR NEWQUAY
An irresistible combination of dramatic coastline, adrenalin sports, gorgeous accommodation and brilliant places to eat and drink.
www.watergatebay.co.uk

Wendy's Coffee Barn
ST AGNES
Barista coffee, wholesome light lunches and delicious homemade cakes all made on site using local produce. Family-friendly and free parking.
www.morgans-online.com/cafe

Wheal Martyn
ST AUSTELL
The unique café is located within the Victorian remains of a china clay settling tank and uses the very best Cornish produce.
www.wheal-martyn.com

Wild Café at Bedruthan Steps
MAWGAN PORTH
A colourful, funky and relaxed place to eat delicious food whilst enjoying watching the beach, the surfers or the sunset.
www.bedruthan.com

Woods Café
BODMIN
A beautiful woodsman's cottage serving homemade lunches and treats every day of the year surrounded by the stunning backdrop of Cardinham Woods.
www.woodscafecornwall.co.uk

ACKNOWLEDGEMENTS

Books like this don't just happen. I am therefore indebted to the following people who have been instrumental in the making of The Great Cornish Food Book:

Rhona Gardiner who convinced me that it could and should happen.

Muse Media for their creative direction, turning our ideas and stories into a thing of beauty.

Rachel Wilson Couch, Jen Eveleigh, Rosie Land, James Land, Grace Lobb, Melodie Manners, Dave Meneer, Heather Mewton, Sadie Phillips, Lia Wall for their contributions, ideas and feedback that helped shape the book.

Dave Huxley for working through countless drafts and challenges with me.

Lindsey Agnew, Tor Amran, Andy Appleton, Andy Atkinson, Aidan Botha, Emilie Calhaem, Steve Chamberlain, Adam Clark, Bill Clarke, Annette Cole, Cornish Mining World Heritage Site, Cornish Pasty Association, Kim Coulson, Adrian Derx, Jean Edwards, Sarah Hayes, Tom Hazzledine, Nick Hemming, Jeremy Hosking, Nick Howell, Meeche Hudd, Tom Hunter, Jason Jobling, Jonathon Jones, Lucy Jones, Bob and Sam Lindo, Frank Linn, Stuart McGuire, Sarah and Tony Marsland, Catherine Mead, Pete Mewton, Mark Muncey, Nathan Outlaw, Angela Parker, Nadia Pendleton, Angela Penrose, Chris Perkins, Philip Pryor, Mark Puckey, Paul Ripley, Gavin Roberts, David Rodda, Nick Rodda, Matthew Rowe (Falmouth Packet Inn), Matthew Rowe (Great Tredinnick Farm), David Simmons, Clare Sivam, Erica Smedley, Tom Sobey, Lara Spurrell, Philip Stansfield, Chris Trenerry, Mark Pitts-Tucker, Ben Tunnicliffe, Paul Wadham, Philip and Ian Warren, Fiona Were, Matthew Wiggins, Vicki Crwys-Williams, Rob Wing: for their time and materials assisting with research and writing of features, photography and verification of facts.

All the other chefs and experts who have allowed us to use their recipes, images and secrets.

The thousands of people who are part of the Cornish food and drink world but not mentioned individually in this book. Together, you all form a world-class industry and Cornwall Food & Drink loves working with you.

Ruth Huxley, August 2013

LIVE IN THE SUNSHINE

swiminthesea

DRINK
IN THE
WILD AIR